Al-Fatihah

The Opening of the Quran
(The Seven Oft-Repeated Ones)

Al-Fatihah

The Opening of the Quran
(The Seven Oft-Repeated Ones)

سورة الفاتحة

(السبع المثاني)

Dr. Shihab M. Ghanem Al Hashmi
Dr. Waddah S. Ghanem Al Hashmi

PARTRIDGE

Print information available on the last page.

Cover Design By Mr. Raed M. Dawood

Publication Approval Awarded 14th February 2016 – National Media Council, Government of the United Arab Emirates.

Approval Reference No: 102297

To order additional copies of this book, contact
Toll Free 800 101 2657 (Singapore)
Toll Free 1 800 81 7340 (Malaysia)
orders.singapore@partridgepublishing.com

www.partridgepublishing.com/singapore

أُدْعُ إِلَىٰ سَبِيلِ رَبِّكَ بِٱلْحِكْمَةِ وَٱلْمَوْعِظَةِ ٱلْحَسَنَةِ وَجَٰدِلْهُم
بِٱلَّتِي هِيَ أَحْسَنُ إِنَّ رَبَّكَ هُوَ أَعْلَمُ بِمَن ضَلَّ عَن سَبِيلِهِۦ وَهُوَ
أَعْلَمُ بِٱلْمُهْتَدِينَ ﴿١٢٥﴾

القرآن الكريم، سورة النحل ، آية 125

Invite to the way of your Lord with wisdom and good instruction,
and argue with them in a way that is best. Indeed, your Lord is most
knowing of who has strayed from His way, and He is most knowing of
who is [rightly] guided. - Nobel Quran, Surat Al Nahl
(The Bee), Ayah (125)

لَآ إِكْرَاهَ فِي ٱلدِّينِ قَد تَّبَيَّنَ ٱلرُّشْدُ مِنَ ٱلْغَيِّ فَمَن يَكْفُرْ
بِٱلطَّٰغُوتِ وَيُؤْمِنۢ بِٱللَّهِ فَقَدِ ٱسْتَمْسَكَ بِٱلْعُرْوَةِ ٱلْوُثْقَىٰ لَا
ٱنفِصَامَ لَهَا وَٱللَّهُ سَمِيعٌ عَلِيمٌ ﴿٢٥٦﴾

القرآن الكريم، سورة البقرة، آية 256

There shall be no compulsion in [acceptance of] the religion.
The right course has become clear from the wrong. So whoever
disbelieves in Taghut and believes in Allah has grasped the most
trustworthy handhold with no break in it. And Allah is Hearing and
Knowing - Nobel Quran, Surat Al Baqarah
(The Cow), Ayah (256)

وَإِذَا سَأَلَكَ عِبَادِى عَنِّى فَإِنِّى قَرِيبٌ أُجِيبُ دَعْوَةَ ٱلدَّاعِ إِذَا دَعَانِ فَلْيَسْتَجِيبُواْ لِى وَلْيُؤْمِنُواْ بِى لَعَلَّهُمْ يَرْشُدُونَ ﴿١٨١﴾

القرآن الكريم، سورة البقرة، آية 186

[*And when My servants ask you,-concerning Me - indeed I am near. I respond to the invocation of the supplicant when he calls upon Me. So let them respond to Me (by obedience) and believe in Me that they may be (rightly) guided.*]
Nobel Quran, Surat Al Baqarah
(The Cow), Ayah (186)

(N.B. The above 3 translations are from Al Sahih International, as published on http://quran.com/)

Dedication

To all humanity, without prejudice

&

*In loving memory of a beloved woman of substance,
Jihad Ali Luqman (born 9th Oct 1950 AD corresponding to
26 Dhul Hijjah 1369 Hijri – died 18th December 2015 AD
corresponding to 7th Rabi ul Awal 1437 Hijri), wife of
Shihab Ghanem and mother of Wiaam,
Waddah and Wajd Shihab Ghanem.*

Contents

Dedication.. ix

Glossary xiii

Foreword (by Dr. M. A. Albar) 1

Authors' Preface 11

Preamble 15

Introduction... 19

Chapter 1:   Legitimacy of the Translation of the Holy Quran 43

Chapter 2:   The Importance of Al-Fatihah 49

Chapter 3:   Al-Istiadah or Seeking Refuge....................................55

Chapter 4:   Al-Basmalah: Bismillahi Ar-Rahman Ar-Raheem 63

Chapter 5:   Al Hamdalah: Al Hamdu Lillah Rabil Alameen............72

Chapter 6:   Ar-Rahman Ar-Raheem...81

Chapter 7:   Maliki Yawm Ad-Deen..88

Chapter 8:   Iyaka Na'budu wa Iyaka Nasta'een 104

Chapter 9:   Ihdina As-Sirat Al-Mustaqeem 118

Chapter 10: Sirat Al-Latheen Anamta Alaihem Ghairi
             Al-Maghdhobi Alaihem wa la Adh-Dhaleen 126

Chapter 11: AMEEN...131

Conclusion...135

List of References and Author's Notes 143

Glossary

Allah	:	The One and Only God
Al-Madinah Al-Munawarah, (also Taibah, also called Yathrib before Islam)	:	The City where the Prophet (PBUH) (ﷺ) established the first Islamic State and where he is buried
As-Sahabah	:	Companions of the Prophet (PBUH) (ﷺ)
Aya, ayah	:	A verse of the Quran. Also a sign of Allah
Ayas, ayat (Plural)	:	Verses of the Quran. Also signs of Allah
Iblis	:	Satan, the Devil
Jibreel (pbuh)	:	Archangel Gabriel. He is the angel of revelation who recited the Quran to the prophet Muhammad (PBUH) (ﷺ) (Trustworthy Ruh/Spirit).
Makkah, (also Mecca)	:	The Holiest City of Islam
Mohammed, Muhammad	:	The final Prophet of Islam, (may the blessings and peace of Allah be upon him)
Mushaf	:	The actual physical Quran book
PBUH, pbuh		Peace be upon him, denoted in Arabic with (ﷺ)

Al-Fatihah

SWT	Subhanaho Wa Ta'ala – Glorified is He (Allah)
Qiblah	The direction towards which a Muslim prays
Quran, Qur'an, (also Koran)	The Holy book of Islam
Sura, surat, suratt, suratth	A chapter of the Holy Quran
Shaitan (plural Shayateen)	Satan, the Devil
Tafseer	Quran interpretation

Foreword

By Dr. Mohammed Ali Albar FRCP (London)
*A founding member of the International Commission on Scientific
Signs Quran and Sunnah, Makkah Al Mukaramah, Saudi Arabia*

بسمـ الله الرحمن الرحيمـ

Bismi Allah Al Rahman Al Rahim

Dr. Shihab Ghanem is an engineer, manager, economist, poet and translator of poetry from Arabic to English and vice versa. He hails from Aden and adopted UAE as his home forty years ago. Here is his profile in a compact nutshell: Born in Aden (1940) into a family of educationists and reformers, son of Muhammad Abduh Ghanem who was a pioneer educationist of Aden and a well known poet in Yemen. His grandfather Abduh Ghanem was a reformer, his maternal grandfather Mohammed Ali Lokman was a towering figure in modern Yemen's history and his maternal uncle Ali M. Luqman was a renowned poet, a politician and editor of both English, and Arabic newspapers in Aden.

A versatile and talented writer Dr. Shihab Ghanem was long ago acknowledged as UAE's leading poet and has carved out a niche for himself in the country's cultural domain. He has been instrumental in cultural give and take between the Arab world and the vast world outside, especially India.

He has published 60 books including 16 books of verse in Arabic and 2 in English and 24 volumes of verse translated from Arabic to English, and from various languages to Arabic via English.

1

Al-Fatihah

He has received various awards including: 1st Prize for Poetry in the UAE (1984), Rashid Award for Scientific Excellence (1989), Book Prize from the Ruler of Sharjah for Poetry Translation (2003 and 2007), Tagore Peace Award (2012/2013), GALA Award (2013), Cultural Personality of the Year Award in Al-Owais Creativity Awards (2013), World Poetry Society Intercontinental Award, Chennai (2013), honouring by Al-Ithnainiah, Jeddah, (2013), Honorary Doctorate in Literature, Japan (2015).

I have known Shihab since we were kids at the primary school of Crater, Aden until we were at the secondary (high) school of Aden college, after which I left for Cairo to study medicine, while he went to the UK and obtained a double degree in Mechanical and Electrical Engineering from Aberdeen. He distinguished himself by obtaining multiple high qualifications in administration and management, a Masters degree in Water Resources Development from Roorkee, India, and a Ph.D. in Economics in Industrialization and Human Resources from Cardiff, U.K. He was the chief editor of World of Engineering, U.A.E. and participated in editing various literary magazines.

Though Dr. Shihab Ghanem, is an engineer, manager and economist by profession, he possesses mastery of verse writing. He was brought up in a literary home with both his father and maternal uncle as eminent poets of Yemen. He himself started to write poems while at Secondary school.

A family of genius brings forth more genius. As a man of literary and poetic abilities, Dr. Shihab became infatuated with the Glorious Qur'an, as he and his son Dr. Waddah mentioned in the introduction.

Dr. Waddah Ghanem is also an environmental engineer, manager and director. He is a passionate researcher and is very interested in comparative religions and philosophy. His current publications are technical papers and text books in the field of health and safety, environment, reflective learning and operational excellence practice. He has to date co-authored three books, published in English in the

U.K. and the U.S.A. and various professional development technical papers and presentations.

The Qur'an with its miraculously eloquent Arabic, challenged the Arabs in their greatest art and expertise. The unbelievers accused the Prophet (ﷺ) of being a poet, a priest, a magician, a madman, and so on. The Qur'an defied them and said that if all humanity plus all the *Jins* tried together, they would fail to produce something like the Qur'an. They could not produce even one *sura* (chapter) like the shortest one with only three verses.

The fact that Quran remains the same text as revealed more than 1400 years ago is in itself a miracle, and it is in the very same words as revealed, with the same pronunciations and recitation of the Prophet Mohammed (ﷺ) and his companions. Muslims believe that other previous scriptures of the People of the Book (Jews, Christians) have been subjected to various corruptions in actual words and meanings.

The Qur'an, which was revealed fourteen centuries ago, mentioned facts only recently discovered or proven by scientists. Dr. Shihab Ghanem and his son Dr. Waddah expounded this point in their marvelous introduction about the Qur'an.

The Glorious Qur'an is the literal word of God, revealed to Mohammed (ﷺ) by the Archangel Gabriel which continued for 23 years (lunar) intermittently from the month of Ramadan (July 609 CE) when Mohammed (ﷺ) reached the age of 40 while he was meditating in the Cave of Hira in a mountain of Makkah (now called Jabel al Noor), until a few months before his death (622 CE).

The first verses (ayas) revealed were the first five verses of Surat Al-Alaq which starts with the word Iqra (Recite/Read) *"Read! In the Name of your Lord, Who has created (all that exists). Has created man from Alaqah (clinging morsel). Read! And your Lord is the Most Generous. Who has taught (the writing) by the pen. Has taught man that which he knew not."* (Q.96:1-5)

Al-Fatihah

The Qur'an is not arranged in chronological order; the verses (ayas) and chapters (suras) were arranged according to the orders of the Prophet Mohammed (ﷺ) himself, which were directed by the Archangel Gabriel as ordained by Allah.

More than half of the Qur'an (19/30) (i.e. 19 parts of the Quran which is in 30 parts) was revealed in Makkah during the first 13 years. The rest (11/30) was revealed in Medina in the last 10 years of the life of the Prophet Mohammed. The suras/chapters of Qur'an revealed in Makkah were usually short suras (chapters) that stressed the dogma of monotheism, the life after death, the Day of Judgment, the salient fundamentals of Islam, while the suras/chapters of Qur'an revealed in Medina came in long chapters (suras) e.g. Al-Baqarah, Aal-Imran, Al-Nisa, Al-Ma'idah and so forth. They have lengthy ayas (verses), regulations of life during war, prohibition of usury, details of how to write and witness contracts, laws of inheritance, prohibition of Al-khamr (intoxicants), certain foods (pork, carrion, blood and whatever is slaughtered for idols). It gives more detail for a settled community with a formation of government, jurisdiction and law.

The Prophet Muhammad (ﷺ) himself did not write or read, but he ordered a group of companions both in Makkah and Medina to write whatever ayas (verses) or suras (chapters) of the Qur'an were revealed. Around 40 of the companions (Sahaba) wrote the Qur'an on leather, parchments, tables of stones (very light stones called pumice from lava of volcanoes of Medina), ribs of palm branches and broad big bones (scapulae) particularly those of camels.

When Abubakr al Siddiq became Khalifa, after the death of the Prophet Mohammed (ﷺ), he waged wars against the apostates of Arabia, and many of those pious men who knew the Qur'an by heart, were killed in the battles. Omar was afraid that the Qur'an would be lost if more of these Sahaba (companions) were killed and suggested the collection of the Qur'an, which Abubakr agreed to and did. The whole collections of parchments, leather, bones, etc. were kept with Hafsa the daughter of

Foreword

Omar who was one of the wives of the Prophet Mohammed (ﷺ). At the time of the third Khalifa Othman bin Affan, some Muslims read the Qur'an and pronounced it in their own dialects (Arab tribes have as many dialects as their number). Othman, gathered the Sahaba (companions) and all agreed to write the Qur'an in accordance with the pronunciation of Quraish, the tribe of the Prophet Mohammed (ﷺ) himself.

Othman commissioned seven copies, and each copy was sent to a certain locality e.g. Egypt, Iraq (Basra & Kofah), Yemen, Makkah and of course Medina. This final compilation of the Qur'an was made in 30H/650 CE. The authors discussed fully the legitimacy of the translation of the Holy Qur'an. Any translation of the Glorious Qur'an, in any language, is not considered Qur'an. It is a translation of the meanings of the Qur'an according to the knowledge and acumen of the translator. It never has the sanctity of the Qur'an, and cannot be used for recitation in prayers. Arabic is the only language of the Qur'an. All Muslims all over the world recite the Qur'an in Arabic in their prayers, and try to understand the meaning in a translation in their language.

Many Muslims, who do not even know Arabic, learn the whole Qur'an by heart and recite it in a beautiful correct recitation! This is one of the wonders of the Holy Qur'an. God, Exalted be His Name, said: "And We have certainly made the Qur'an easy for remembrance; so is there any who will remember?".)Q.54:17)

The beauty of the language of the Qur'an is immutable and can not be replicated, and its rhythm is suitable for remarkably beautiful recitations, admired by even those who do not know Arabic. The art of calligraphy was created by the Qur'an's writers.

The Qur'an is the soul of the Muslim, and the center of his artistic activities. At the same time, the text from which all the ahkam (rulings) of Islamic jurisprudence are derived from the Qur'an and the Sunna (the traditions) of the Prophet Mohammed (ﷺ), by the most prominent learned people of Islam.

Al-Fatihah

Muslims believe that all communities received Allah's guidance through revelation given to the Prophets and Messengers of Allah. In Islam, Adam is not only the first human being; he is also the first Prophet who delivered Allah's message of monotheism to his descendants.

It is important to state from the outset that Muslims do not believe in "the original sin". Adam committed an act of disobedience by eating from the fruit of the tree which Allah had ordered him not to eat. According to the Qur'an, he and his wife, Eve, repented and God accepted their repentance and they became pure. God bestowed on Adam and Eve and their children His Grace and Blessing *"We honored the progeny of Adam, provided them with transport on land and sea; given them for sustenance things good and pure; and conferred on them special favors above a great part of Our creation"* (Qur'an/17:70).

Furthermore, Muslims believe that God sent prophets and messengers to every nation and people to guide them to worship one God and follow the path of righteousness. It is significant to note that, as the youngest of the monotheistic traditions, Islam addresses the whole of humanity and respects all the prophets from Adam to the last Prophet Muhammad and considers all nations to have witnessed Allah's uncompromising unity confirmed in all the messages and teaching of God's true envoys on earth. Belief in God's unity (*Tawhid*) is the basis not only for Muslim theology; but it is also the basis of morality and ethics in Islam.

The Qur'an mentions a number of prophets and apostles, for instance Noah (Nuh), Abraham (Ibrahim), Ishmael (Ismail), Isaac (Ishaq), Jacob (Ya'qub/Israel), Joseph (Yusuf), Moses (Musa), Zacaria (Zakariyah), Jesus (Isa), John the Baptist(Yahya), Jonah (Yunus), Lot and so on.

"Say we believe in God, and His revelation given to us, and to Abraham, Ishmael, Isaac, Jacob, and the Tribes (The 12 tribes of Israel i.e the offspring of the 12 sons of Jacob (PBUH)) and that given to Moses and Jesus, and that given to all prophets from their Lord. We make no

difference between one and another of them; and we bow to God in submission (Islam)". (Q. 2:136)

"The Apostle believes in what has been revealed to him from His Lord; as do the men of faith. Each one of them believes in Allah, His Angels, His books and His Apostles. We make no distinction between one and another of His Apostles. And they say we hear, we obey; we seek your forgiveness, our Lord, and to You is the return (of all)". (Q. 2:285).

The Qur'an orders Muslims to argue other faiths with respect and friendly attitude, *"Do not argue with the People of the Scriptures except in the most kindly manner-unless it be such of them as are set on evil doing- and say: We believe in that which has been bestowed upon us, as well as that which was bestowed upon you; for our God and your God is one and the same, and unto Him that we surrender ourselves".* (Q. 29:46) Indeed, the religion of God introduced the compassionate ethos which was the hallmark of the more advanced religion: brotherhood and social justice were its crucial virtues. A strong egalitarianism would continue to characterize the Islamic ideal.

Islam is the religion that unites all of humanity from Adam till doomsday and considers all nations to have witnessed One God through the messages and teachings of their respective prophets:

"There is no nation that was not given an admonisher". (Q. 35:24).

All people are the progeny of Adam who was elevated to be the vicegerent of God on earth.

The unity of human beings is established in many verses of the Qur'an and the traditions of the Prophet Muhammed (ﷺ). The value of a human being depends on his good deeds, and not on his wealth or position:

"Oh mankind, We created you from a single (pair) of a male and female, and made you into nations and tribes that you may know each other.

Al-Fatihah

Verily the most honored of you in the sight of Allah (God) is he who is the most righteous of you. Verily Allah is All-Knowing". (Q. 49:13).

Every Muslim has to surrender himself/herself in obeisance to Allah, The Creator, The Sovereign, The Merciful, the Exalted who has ninety-nine beautiful names and attributes, which were fully explained by the authors of this book.

In the Qur'an, Allah is more impersonal than Yahweh of the Torah ...We can only glimpse something of God in the signs of nature, and so transcendent is He that we can only talk about Him in parables. Therefore, the Qur'an constantly urges Muslims to see the world as a clear sign of God's Omniscience and Omnipotence: *"Verily in the creation of the heavens and of the earth and the succession of night and day in the ships that speed through the sea with what is useful to mankind; and in the waters which God sends down from the sky, giving life thereby to the earth after it had been lifeless, and causing all manner of living creatures to multiply there on; and in the change of the winds, and the clouds that run their appointed courses between sky and earth. (In all this) there are signs, indeed for people who use their reason".* (Q. 2/164).

The Qur'an constantly stresses the need for intelligence in deciphering the "signs" or "messages" of God. Muslims are not to abdicate their reason, but are to look at the world attentively and with curiosity. It was this attitude that enabled Muslims to build a fine tradition of natural science, which has never been seen as such a danger to religion as in Christianity (e.g. during the dark ages). A study of the workings of the natural world showed that it had a transcendent dimension and source, which we can talk about only in signs and symbols; even the stories of the prophets, the accounts of the Last Judgment, and the joys of Paradise should not be interpreted literally, but as parables of higher ineffable reality." The Prophet said that Jannah i.e. Paradise is something that no eye has seen or heard of or even crosses the imagination of any human being.

Foreword

The Qur'an emphatically denied any association with God, neither as wife or son:

"Say: He is the One God, the Eternal Refuge (the uncaused cause of all beings). He begets not, and neither is He begotten, and there is nothing that could be compared to Him" (Q.112:1-4).

"That is God (Allah), your Lord, the Creator of all things, so worship Him, and He is the Disposer of all things. Vision perceives Him not, but He perceives all vision, and He is the Subtle (above all comprehension) yet acquainted with all things" (Q. 6:102-103).

By contemplating the signs (ayas) of nature and the verses of the Qur'an, Muslims could glimpse that aspect of divinity…we only see God through His activities, which adapt His Ineffable being to our limited understanding. The Qur'an urges Muslims to cultivate perpetual consciousness (taqwa) of the Face or the Self of God that surrounds them on all sides *"Wheresoever you turn, there is the Face of Allah (and He is above, over His throne). Surely Allah is All-Sufficient for His creatures' needs, All-Knowing."* (Q. 2:115). The Qur'an sees God as the Absolute, Who alone has True Existence.

The Qur'an stressed the continuity of the religious experience of humankind, and teaches that God sent Messengers to every people on the face of the earth.

After discussing the difficulty in translating the Glorious Qur'an into other languages, and that any translation is not considered Qur'an, the authors stressed that translation of the meanings of the Glorious Qur'an is essential to propagate the word of God, and let all people have a fair idea about the Qur'an and its teachings.

They went into deep study of the exegesis and commentaries of *Al-Fatihah*, the opening chapter of the Glorious Qur'an. They gave a detailed study of its importance, as it should be recited by every Muslim, at least 17 times daily in the five different prayers dawn (Fajr) to night prayer (Isha).

No prayer is complete without reading (reciting) Al-Fatihah.

They went through more than thirty English translations and were satisfied many a time by the Arabic Qur'anic word, which was explained in one or more paragraphs.

Their work is really stupendous, as it required mastery of Arabic and English languages plus deep rooted knowledge of the multitude of Tafsir (exegesis) and commentaries of eminent Islamic scholars throughout the ages.

It is a wonderful feat accomplished by a versatile and talented writer, an outstanding poet and unsurpassed translator of poetry from many languages to Arabic via English and vice versa.

His eloquence and taste of the beauty of the language drew him and his son Dr. Waddah to the Glorious Qur'an, the apogee of eloquence in Arabic language.

Their deep study which continued for many years brings to the readers a masterpiece of work to enjoy the beauty of the Qur'an represented by Al-Fatiha, the opening sura (chapter) of the Glorious Qur'an. Though it is only seven ayas (verses), it encapsulates the major aims and parts of the whole Qur'an.

Dr. Shihab Ghanam and his son Dr. Waddah masterfully introduce the English reader to the Al-Fatiha, its wonders and its beauty as a representative of the whole Qur'an.

Dr. Mohammed Ali Albar,
Ramadan 1436 - June 2015
Jeddah, Kingdon of Saudia Arabia

Authors' Preface

All absolute and perfect praise is to the one and only God, Allah, and may the blessings be bestowed on His messenger Muhammad, peace be upon him and his progeny, companions and followers. Al-Fatihah is a significantly important chapter, as it is not only the opening chapter and the essence and abstract of the Holy Quran, it is the sura which is used in every mandatory and voluntary prayer.

This book was written with the primary objective of explaining in detail, but as concisely as possible, the first sura (chapter) of the Holy Quran: Al-Fatihah, "the Opening". This book has been written over a period of many years and both the authors, a father and a son, have travelled a most significant journey to get to the point of developing this publication. Earlier versions of some of the chapters were published a few years ago in Islamic magazines such as Radiance of India.

From the very start our motivation has been to render a clear and concise explanation of this sura which is very dear, not only to our hearts, but to the heart of every practicing Muslim. We have spent many hours through this journey discussing and debating more than 30 published translation attempts and made our own attempt based on the interpretations of these seven most oft-repeated verses. We have in the process depended mainly on the interpretations of both classical and contemporary mainstream scholars whom we felt provided great insights with a balanced and sound interpretation based on both solid linguistic and most widely accepted reference positions.

Whilst Al-Fatihah and the Holy Quran are wonderfully philosophical, we have avoided delving into the more philosophical discourses and debates, and focused on the clear and very apparent interpretation. We felt that some depth of research was required to explain Al-Fatihah, but we did not see the value in producing a book in English which was complex and very wordy and that could lead to confusion rather than providing an easy access to a mainstream explanation of Al-Fatihah.

Whilst the concepts of Al-Fatihah are ultimately simple, uncomplicated and straight forward - this does not mean that the same very concepts are not very deep indeed. We have thus tried to provide that clear picture of Al-Fatihah themes as debated by the most learned scholars of *Tafseer (i.e Quran interpretation)*.

We also wanted to provide a book which allowed both Muslims and non-Muslims who are neither native in Arabic nor competent in reading and understanding Arabic, to access this absolutely purposeful set of Quranic verses. We believe Al-Fatihah answers many very foundational and critical questions for mankind – and we believe that the Almighty summarized for mankind "their purpose and mission" in the 7 oft repeated verses.

No other project that we have done in the past few years, or probably at any time in our lives has made us think deeply and reflect as much as this book has. We only hope that we have done Al-Fatihah justice; and that we have contributed a little to bringing both Muslims and non-Muslims closer to understanding this magnificent chapter and that this book is a small step on the road of the dialogue of civilizations. We therefore invite the reader to study this book with an open mind, an open heart and a positive outlook to a better understanding of Al-Fatihah, the Quran and Islam.

Finally, we would like to thank Eng. Alia Mubarak Busamara and her sister Haifa Mubarak Busamra; Mr. Barry Bell and others for their valuable review and comments. We would also like to thank our family members for their support over the years during our work on this book.

Authors' Preface

May the Almighty accept from us all.

Dr. Shihab M. Ghanem & Dr. Waddah S. Ghanem
Al-Muharram 1437 - November 2015
Dubai, United Arab Emirates

Preamble

Al-Fatihah whilst being a very short chapter contains the essence of the Quran. The concepts of Allah being the source of endless mercy; the praise of the Lord; the Lord of All Worlds and the Sovereign Master of the day of reckoning and recompense; The Solely Worshiped; The Solely Ultimately Depended on; and the Only One Who can lead all creation to the straight and righteous path are wonderfully summarized in the 7 verses containing 29 words and 139 Arabic letters.

This book comes in 13 chapters (Introduction, earlier parts and the Conclusion are not included in this number). After this preamble which gives the outline of the book, comes an introduction about the Holy Quran which discusses why the Quran was revealed as the final message in Arabia. As this book attempts to provide as accurate an approximate translation as possible based on the research undertaken, the legitimacy of the translation of the Holy Quran is discussed in chapter 1.

In the second chapter, *Al-Fatihah* and its significance and importance are addressed. This is followed by the seeking of refuge in Allah from the devil in a the third chapter entitled the *Al-Istiadah*. Chapter 4 discusses the *Al-Basmalah*, which is reading in the Name of Allah. In Chapter 5 we discuss the verse of praise, *Al-Hamdalah*. This is then followed in Chapter 6 by the greatest of attributes of the Lord: *Ar-Rahman Ar-Raheem*.

One of the longest chapters in this book is Chapter 7. This chapter discusses Allah as the Sovereign Master of the Day of Recompense, in *Maliki* Yawm-id-Deen. The central point of Al-Fatihah follows in

Chapter 8 in *Iyaka Na'budu wa Iyaka Nasta'een*, where the very heart of monotheistic belief lies. In Chapter 9 the straight path in *Ihdina As-Sirat Al-Mustaqeem is discussed*, followed in Chapter 10 by a discussion of those who are on that path in *Sirat al-Latheen Anamta Alaihem Ghairi Al-Maghdhobi Alaihem wa la Adh-Dhaleen*. That ends *Al-Fathiha*, but in Chapter 11, very briefly *Ameen is discussed*. In the final concluding part of this book, a suggested translation is presented with some final reflections.

We hope that this book will help its readers to understand Al-Fatihah better and therefore the Quran and Islam. In this study we have tried as much as possible to use mainstream classical and contemporary interpretations and writings in the very spirit of the Quranic verse:

وَكَذَٰلِكَ جَعَلْنَٰكُمْ أُمَّةً وَسَطًا لِّتَكُونُوا۟ شُهَدَآءَ عَلَى ٱلنَّاسِ وَيَكُونَ ٱلرَّسُولُ عَلَيْكُمْ شَهِيدًا ۗ وَمَا جَعَلْنَا ٱلْقِبْلَةَ ٱلَّتِي كُنتَ عَلَيْهَآ إِلَّا لِنَعْلَمَ مَن يَتَّبِعُ ٱلرَّسُولَ مِمَّن يَنقَلِبُ عَلَىٰ عَقِبَيْهِ ۚ وَإِن كَانَتْ لَكَبِيرَةً إِلَّا عَلَى ٱلَّذِينَ هَدَى ٱللَّهُ ۗ وَمَا كَانَ ٱللَّهُ لِيُضِيعَ إِيمَٰنَكُمْ ۚ إِنَّ ٱللَّهَ بِٱلنَّاسِ لَرَءُوفٌ رَّحِيمٌ ﴿١٤٣﴾

(البقرة/143)

"And thus we have made you a middle-nation (a just community) that you will be witnesses over mankind and the Messenger will be a witness over you. And We did not make the Qiblah which you used to face except that We might make evident who would follow the Messenger from who would turn back on his heels. And indeed, it is difficult except for those whom Allah has guided. And never would Allah have caused you to lose your faith. Indeed Allah is, to the people, Kind and Merciful."

Surat Al Baqarah (The Cow), Ayah 143. [1]

Preamble

Islam was never a religion for just one people, one nation or one race, it was, is, and will always be an open invitation for the whole of mankind to be as one, and rejoice in the Mercy of the One and Only God. It is a way of life. Although it lays great importance on the spiritual life of a person, it also lays importance to the present life. This can be seen from the following two verses of the Quran:

وَلَلْأَخِرَةُ خَيْرٌ لَّكَ مِنَ ٱلْأُولَىٰ ٤

(الضحى/4)

"And the Hereafter is better for you than the first (life)." - Surat Al Duha, Ayah 4 [2].

وَٱبْتَغِ فِيمَآ ءَاتَىٰكَ ٱللَّهُ ٱلدَّارَ ٱلْءَاخِرَةَ وَلَا تَنسَ نَصِيبَكَ مِنَ ٱلدُّنْيَا وَأَحْسِن كَمَآ أَحْسَنَ ٱللَّهُ إِلَيْكَ وَلَا تَبْغِ ٱلْفَسَادَ فِى ٱلْأَرْضِ إِنَّ ٱللَّهَ لَا يُحِبُّ ٱلْمُفْسِدِينَ ٧٧

(القصص/77)

"But seek, through that which Allah has given you, the abode of the Hereafter; and (yet), do not forget your share of the world. And do good as Allah has done good to you. And seek not corruption in the land. Indeed, Allah does not like corrupters."
- Surat Al Qasas, Ayah 77 [3].

It is to this end worthy to note that when the Prophet (ﷺ) migrated to Yathrib (later called Al-Madinah Al-Munawarah, Taibah) in 622 A.D. one of the first things he did was to establish together with Jews, other non-Muslims as well as Muslims, the *Wathiqa of Al-Madinah*, i.e. The Document of Al-Madinah, which was the first constitution in human history in which all the citizens of Al-Madinah had equal rights and responsibilities irrespective of race, colour or creed.

This stands today as one of the greatest testemonies in history of Islam's inherent message of equality to all mankind.

Introduction

It is said by many Muslims today that Islam is the most misunderstood religion. But also Islam is the fastest spreading religion, despite the fact that most of the Muslim countries are part of the poorer third world. This apparently paradoxical picture deserves to be examined. It seems that whenever Islam is accused by its opponents, more people embrace Islam. The Quran states clearly:

يُرِيدُونَ أَن يُطْفِئُوا نُورَ ٱللَّهِ بِأَفْوَٰهِهِمْ وَيَأْبَى ٱللَّهُ إِلَّا أَن يُتِمَّ نُورَهُۥ وَلَوْ كَرِهَ ٱلْكَٰفِرُونَ ﴿٣٢﴾

(التوبة/32)

"Fain would they extinguish Allah's Light with their mouths, but Allah will not allow but that His Light should be perfected, even though the Unbelievers may detest (it)"
- Surat Al Tawbah, Ayah 32. [4]

The main purpose of this book is to give a concise interpretation of Al-Fatihah, the seven-verse Opening chapter of the Nobel, Glorious, Holy Quran, القرآن الكريم. But in this introduction a short note about the Quran itself, the holy scripture of Islam, and the circumstances of its revelation will be presented as a background to this book.

The Quran is a medium sized book in Arabic, usually written in calligraphy. A widely circulated print copy, of which there are millions of copies all over the world, reprinted every year by the Saudi Arabian government is just over 600 pages. The book is in 30 more or less equal

19

parts. It has 114 Chapters varying in length. The longest chapter, Surat Al-Baqara (i.e. the Cow) has 286 ayas or verses, while the shortest chapters have only three verses. There are three such chapters but the shortest in number of words is Al-Kawther. The total number of verses in the Quran according to the *Mushaf* of Al-Madinah Al-Munawwarah (i.e. the Quran as printed and published there) is 6236. According to the interpretation of the Quran by Abu Bakr Jaber Al-Jaza'iri titled Aysar At-Tafasir li Kalam Al-'Ali Al-Qadeer, the number ranges between 6204 and 6240 according to the different schools of recitation and the places of the fullstops. But the actual words of all versions are the same.

Unlike the Holy Bible, there is only one version of the Quran, and it is accepted by Muslims of all sects and schools of thought. Only the Arabic version is considered as Quran, and is accepted as the actual words of Allah as revealed to Prophet Muhammad (ﷺ) as conveyed to him by Jibreel (Archangel Gabriel) (PBUH). All translations in all other languages are merely human efforts to interpret the meanings of the words of the Quran as concisely as possible.

The Quran was revealed gradually in small parts over a period of 23 years, 13 in Makkah Al-Mukarramah (Mecca) from the day the Prophet (ﷺ) was made the Messenger of Allah in Ghar Hira (the Cave of Hira) at the age of forty, and 10 years during the period from his Hijra (migration) to Al-Madinah Al-Munawwarah (Medina) until he passed away at the age of 63 Hijri years. The suras that were revealed before the Hijra are known as the Makkian (or Meccian) suras. They are 82 in number and tend to have short verses. The suras that were revealed after the Hijra are known as the Madinian suras. They are 20 in number but tend to be longer and to have longer verses. There are also 12 suras, including Al-Fatihah, around which there is controversy in whether to consider them Makkian or Madenian.

Generally speaking the Makkian suras tend to focus on questions and topics related to faith; the Hereafter and Paradise and Hellfire; the stories of the previous prophets such as Noah (PBUH), Ibrahim (i.e. Abraham) (PBUH), Musa (i.e Moses) (PBUH) and Isa (i.e Jesus) (PBUH). A total of 25 prophets are mentioned by name in the Quran but the Quran also mentions that there were many more. The Makkian suras also focus on the wrong deeds of the unbelievers such as worshipping idols, burying some of their newborn daughters alive, appropriating the property or money of orphans, warring and blood shedding for no legitimate reason; etc. The Madinian suras generally focus more on questions and subjects related to worship practice and procedures, transactions; *halal* and *haram* i.e. what is permitted and what is not permitted in Islam; the rules of the *greater jihad* (inner struggle of the self) and the *minor jihad* (fight in the cause of justice and defence against aggression against Islam), and war and peace; jurisprudence and its aims and what is ordained, family laws, and the laws of punishments for various crimes, etc. These Madenian suras also speak about the hypocrites and religious arguments with the people of the Book (i.e. Jews and Christians); etc.

Some of the unbelievers at the time of the Prophet (ﷺ) questioned why the Quran was not revealed in one go. This is mentioned in the Quran, which also gave the answer:

وَقَالَ ٱلَّذِينَ كَفَرُوا۟ لَوْلَا نُزِّلَ عَلَيْهِ ٱلْقُرْءَانُ جُمْلَةً وَٰحِدَةً ۚ كَذَٰلِكَ لِنُثَبِّتَ بِهِۦ فُؤَادَكَ ۖ وَرَتَّلْنَٰهُ تَرْتِيلًا ﴿٣٢﴾

"Those who reject Faith say: "Why is not the Quran revealed to him all at once? Thus (is it revealed), that We may strengthen thy heart thereby, and We have recited (rehearsed) it to thee in slow, well-arranged stages, gradually."

Surat Al Furqan, Ayah 32. [5]

The Prophet (ﷺ) belonged to the tribe of Quraish, the influential Arab tribe which lived in Makkah Al-Mukaramah. From his youth he was always known to his people since to be of superior personal character, and was referred to as Al-Ameen, i.e. The Honest or Trustworthy. He was 25 years old when Quraish were about to fight amongst themselves about who was to have the great honour of placing the Black Stone in the corner of the Kabaa, which was the greatest shrine of the Arabs during Jahiliyah, the period before Islam, and it is the greatest shrine of Muslims since the advent of Islam to the present day. This was during one of the re-buildings of the Kaaba which was there since time immemorial, and was rebuilt after that by Prophet Ibrahim (ﷺ) (Abraham) with the help of his son Prophet Ismail (Ishmael) (ﷺ). To avoid a fight, the leaders of Quraish agreed to ask the first person to enter the Haram (the area around the Kaaba) to make the decision and abide by his decision. The person who entered was none other than Muhammad (ﷺ). They were very pleased as he was known for his honesty and sagacity. He asked them to bring a cloak and place the Black Stone in its middle and asked each group/tribe to take hold of part of the cloak and lift it up to the level where the stone was to be placed. He then took the stone himself and put it in its place. Everyone was happy with the outcome as they all participated, and conflict was avoided.

Muhammad (ﷺ) was always a God-fearing and pious person. He used to take food and water and go to a cave outside Makkah to meditate about the Universe and its Creator, etc. for several days and nights at a time. Once at the age of forty during the month of Ramadan whilst in that cave Jibreel (PBUH) appeared to him and said to him: "Read!". Muhammad (ﷺ), trembling in fear said that he could not read for he had not learnt to read and write. Jibreel hugged him so tightly that Muhammad (ﷺ)could not bear it anymore and then Jibreel released him and repeated the command: "Read!". This was repeated three times. Muhammaad (ﷺ) asked what was it that he had to read. Then Jibreel (ﷺ) recited the first five verses of Surat Al-Alaq:

$$ ﴿ اقْرَأْ بِاسْمِ رَبِّكَ الَّذِي خَلَقَ ١ ﴾ $$

(العلق/1)

22

$$خَلَقَ ٱلْإِنسَـٰنَ مِنْ عَلَقٍ ٢$$

(العلق/2)

$$ٱقْرَأْ وَرَبُّكَ ٱلْأَكْرَمُ ٣$$

(العلق/3)

$$ٱلَّذِى عَلَّمَ بِٱلْقَلَمِ ٤$$

(العلق/4)

$$عَلَّمَ ٱلْإِنسَـٰنَ مَا لَمْ يَعْلَمْ ٥$$

(العلق/5)

"Recite in the name of your Lord who created"
"Created man from a clinging substance"
"Recite, and your Lord is the most Generous".
"Who taught by the pen".
"Taught man that which he knew not"

Surat Al –Alaq, 1-5. [6]

These were the first ayas or verses of the Quran revealed to the Prophet (ﷺ) who had become effectively at that moment the last Messenger of Allah. He went home terrified and shivering, and asked his beloved wife Khadijah to cover him and she covered him with a cloak. When he settled down he recounted to her the experience and was worried that something was wrong with him but she immediately reassured him saying:

فقالت خديجة: لَا وَاللَّهِ مَا يُخْزِيكَ اللَّهُ أَبَدًا إِنَّكَ لَتَصِلُ الرَّحِمَ وَتَحْمِلُ الْكَلَّ وَتَكْسِبُ الْمَعْدُومَ وَتَقْرِي الضَّيْفَ وَتُعِينُ عَلَى نَوَائِبِ الْحَقِّ (رواه البخاري)

i.e. Khadjah (MABPWH) said: *"Never! By Allah, Allah will never disgrace you. You keep good relations with your kith and kin, help the poor and the destitute, serve your guests generously and assist the deserving calamity-afflicted ones."* (Narrated by Al-Bukhari). [7]

She then accompanied him to her cousin Waraqa bin Naufal who, during the pre-Islamic period had become a Christian and used to write the Gospel in Hebrew letters. At the time of their visit he was an old man who had lost his eyesight. After Muhammad (ﷺ) told him what had happened to him Waraqa said that the Prophet (ﷺ) had just received the beginning of the message through the same Angel that delivered the message to Moses and other prophets and anticipated that Quraish would oppose him harshly and drive him out of Makkah. Waraqa said that if he lived until that day he would support him strongly, but Warqa died a few days after that incident.

Sometimes people wonder why the message of Islam was revealed in Arabic to an illiterate Arab in the Arabian Peninsula. To begin with we should explain that the basic message of Islam is to believe in a One and Only Creator and to surrender oneself to Him and worship Him alone without *shirk* i.e. polytheism. The word "Islam" in Arabic means to surrender. It is the blinding pride of man that has blurred his vision to understanding this basic and natural concept, and to be subservient to Allah his Creator. Prophets before Prophet Muhammad (ﷺ) were sent to their own people whereas Muhammad (ﷺ) was sent to all humanity. The Quran states:

وَمَآ أَرْسَلْنَكَ إِلَّا كَآفَّةً لِّلنَّاسِ بَشِيرًا وَنَذِيرًا وَلَكِنَّ
أَكْثَرَ النَّاسِ لَا يَعْلَمُونَ ﴿٢٨﴾

(سبأ/28)

[And We have not sent you except comprehensively (a universal
Messenger) to mankind as a bringer of glad (good) tidings and a
forewarner. But most of the people do not know.]

Surat Saba, Ayah 28 [8]

In fact the message delivered by Muhammad (ﷺ) is to both human beings and to the Jinn. Both these beings are the only creatures of Allah that have been given a choice of decision regarding their actions, and thus unlike the angels and all other creatures of Allah. But the Messenger was also sent as a mercy to all creatures. The Quran states:

وَمَآ أَرْسَلْنَكَ إِلَّا رَحْمَةً لِّلْعَالَمِينَ ﴿١٠٧﴾

(الأنبياء/ 107)

"And We have not sent you, [O Muhammad], except as a mercy
to the worlds."

Surat Al Anbiya (The Prophets), Ayah 107. [9].

In fact Muslims believe that all prophets of Allah actually conveyed the message of Islam: belief in the one and only God and the surrender to Him. The message delivered by Muhammad (ﷺ) is the final comprehensive message which beside carrying the same message of the unity of God and surrendering to Him elaborates the codes for living in this World in order to deserve entering Paradise. It completes and supersedes all previous messages.

When the Quran was revealed to Muhammad (ﷺ); humanity had reached the point of maturity to receive the final detailed message of Islam. Allah had provided the right messenger, with the highest required character and morals, and protected him until he delivered the whole and complete message, then shortly after that he made him pass away, for humanity to continue implementing the message. The Quran states the following verses:

$$\text{وَإِنَّكَ لَعَلَى خُلُقٍ عَظِيمٍ} \quad ٤$$

(القلم/4)

"And indeed, you are of a great moral character."
Surat Al Qalam (The Pen), Ayah 4 [10]

$$\text{يَا أَيُّهَا الرَّسُولُ بَلِّغْ مَا أُنزِلَ إِلَيْكَ مِن رَّبِّكَ وَإِن لَّمْ تَفْعَلْ فَمَا بَلَّغْتَ رِسَالَتَهُ وَاللَّهُ يَعْصِمُكَ مِنَ النَّاسِ إِنَّ اللَّهَ لَا يَهْدِي الْقَوْمَ الْكَافِرِينَ} \quad ٦٧$$

(المائدة/67)

"O Messenger, announce that which has been revealed to you from your Lord, and if you do not, then you have not conveyed His message. And Allah will protect you from the people. Indeed, Allah does not guide the disbelieving people."
Surat Al Ma'eda, Ayah 67. [11]

At the beginning Islam spread very slowly. The Quran instructed the Prophet (ﷺ) to begin spreading the message first among his relatives and kinsmen:

$$\text{وَأَنذِرْ عَشِيرَتَكَ الْأَقْرَبِينَ} \quad ٢١٤$$

(الشعراء/214)

"And warn, [O Muhammad], your closest kindred."
Surat Ash-Shu'ara', Ayah 214. [12].

By Hijat Al-Wada, the Farewell Pilgrimage which was the last but also only pilgrimage of the Prophet (ﷺ) after Hijra (on the 10th year of Hijra), and the Quran stated that the religion of Islam had been finally perfected:

$$...الْيَوْمَ أَكْمَلْتُ لَكُمْ دِينَكُمْ وَأَتْمَمْتُ عَلَيْكُمْ نِعْمَتِي وَرَضِيتُ$$

$$لَكُمُ الْإِسْلَامَ دِينًا$$

(المائدة/3)

[......This day have I perfected your religion for you, completed My favour upon you, and have chosen for you Islam as your religion....]
Surat Al-Ma'idah Ayah 3) [13]

The number of Muslims at the time of the Hijra to Al-Madinah, about 13 years after the beginning of the revelation of the Quran, was quite small, not exceeding a few hundred at the most. Today it is estimated that there are 1.6 billion Muslims, and Islam is expected to become the religion with the largest following in the world within the next few decades, not only through a higher rate of birth, but also through a higher rate of conversion to Islam in the West and other parts of the world. The Quran says:

$$هُوَ الَّذِى أَرْسَلَ رَسُولَهُ بِالْهُدَى وَدِينِ الْحَقِّ لِيُظْهِرَهُ عَلَى الدِّينِ كُلِّهِ وَلَوْ كَرِهَ الْمُشْرِكُونَ ۝$$

(الصف/9)

Al-Fatihah

"It is He who has sent His Messenger with guidance and the religion of truth to manifest it over all religion, although they who associate other dieties with Allah dislike it."

Surat Al Saf, Ayah 9 [14]

The Prophet (ﷺ) said:

"والله ليتمن الله هذا الأمر حتى يسير الراكب من صنعاء إلى حضرموت لا

يخاف إلا الله والذئب على غنمه، ولكنكم تستعجلون" (رواه البخاري)

"By Allah! This religion (Islam) will be completed (and triumph) till a rider (traveler) goes from San`a' (the capital of Yemen) to Hadramout fearing nobody except Allah and the wolf lest it should trouble his sheep, but you are impatient". (Narrated by Al-Bukhari) [15]

The Prophet (ﷺ) also said:

"لَيَبْلُغَنَّ هَذَا الْأَمْرُ مَا بَلَغَ اللَّيْلُ وَالنَّهَارُ وَلَا يَتْرُكُ اللَّهُ بَيْتَ مَدَرٍ وَلَا وَبَرٍ إِلَّا

أَدْخَلَهُ اللَّهُ هَذَا الدِّينَ." (مسند أحمد)

"i.e. This matter will reach where night and day reach and Allah will not leave a house made of clay or camel hair without this religion entering it." (Narrated by Ahmed) [16]

Several factors were behind the success of the spread of Islam including the existence of the right great leader, Prophet Muhammad (ﷺ); the great message in the form of the Glorious Quran; and the Hadith and traditions and explanations of the Messenger (ﷺ), and also the core of great early Muslims who made huge sacrifices to carry the message in its earlier years. The Creator (SWT) who controls the scheme of all things, provided all the necessary (enabeling) factors. We have already spoken briefly about the role of the Prophet (ﷺ).

Introduction

We will speak now about the role played by the men of the Peninsula at the time of the Prophet (ﷺ).

The Arabs of the Peninsula were the first people to receive the message. They lived largely in a desert type of environment which influenced their character. At the time the message reached them they were generally idol worshippers. In fact one of the main reasons why Quraish, the tribe of the Prophet (ﷺ), opposed Islam was because Makkah had become the center of pilgrimage of the Arabs of the Peninsula to the large number of idols inside and around the Ka'ba, from which activity Quraish gained commercially.

Some of the Arabs of the Peninsula used to bury their female newborns alive for fear that they may be taken as slave girls by raiding tribes, or for fear that they would become wives of persons of lesser status, or because the poorer fathers feared having to provide for them.

The Quran states:

وَإِذَا بُشِّرَ أَحَدُهُم بِالْأُنثَىٰ ظَلَّ وَجْهُهُ مُسْوَدًّا وَهُوَ كَظِيمٌ ۝

(النحل 58)

"And when one of them is informed of [the birth of] a female, his face becomes dark, and he suppresses grief."
Surat Al Nahal (The Bee), Ayah 58

يَتَوَارَىٰ مِنَ الْقَوْمِ مِن سُوءِ مَا بُشِّرَ بِهِ أَيُمْسِكُهُ عَلَىٰ هُونٍ أَمْ يَدُسُّهُ فِي التُّرَابِ أَلَا سَاءَ مَا يَحْكُمُونَ ۝

(النحل 59)

29

"He hides himself from the people because of the ill of which he has been informed. Should he keep it in humiliation or bury it in the ground? Unquestionably, evil is what they decide."

Surat Al Nahal (The Bee), Ayah 59 [17].

It is worthy to note that forms of female infanticide are sadly enough still practiced today in some countries. The Wikipedia defines female infanticide as: *"the deliberate killing of newborn female children. In countries with a history of female infanticide, the modern practice of sex-selective abortion is often discussed as a closely related issue. Female infanticide is a major cause of concern in several nations such as China and India. It has been argued that the "low status" in which women are viewed in patriarchal societies creates a bias against females."*

The Arabs of the peninsula were warring tribes that attacked one another sometimes for trivial reasons and in some cases their tribal wars continued for decades like the War of Al-Basoos around 494 A.D., which was started by Kulaib, the head of a tribe, killing a camel from another tribe which was grazing with his camels in his grazing ground! The war lasted more than two decades and some say 40 years. Another war was called Dahes and Al-Ghabra named after two horses belonging to the leaders of two tribes which were raced together and there was accusation of foul play. This war also lasted around 40 years!

Debauchery and drinking alcohol in excess were not considered sins at the time. On the contrary they were a source of pride to some of those Arabs. The famous Jahili (pre-Islamic) poet Tarafa bin Al-Abd says in his *mu'alaqa* (a poem hung in the Ka'ba because of its great status) that except for three things he did not care to live. These were drinking, women, and fighting in support of those who asked him to help them against injustice and aggression. It is this spirit of chivalry in the seven (some say ten) Mu'allaqat (odes) and other pre-Islamic poetry that fascinated several (European) orientalist scholars. Beside chivalry the pre-Islamic Arabs were famous for exceptional bravery, extreme generosity and hospitality, pride and self-esteem, keeping promises and words of honour even at the cost of their own lives, loving and respecting parents and relatives, and various other outstanding high morals which are evident in their poetry and many incidents in their history. The harsh desert environment conditioned them to living with minimum food with dates as one of their basic diets, and also with minimum water. One of their well-known sayings states: "We are a people who do not eat unless hungry, and when we eat we don't do it to satiation". Their appreciation of the predicament of thirst and hunger made them very generous and hospitable to others including absolute strangers. Hospitality and generosity are highly spoken of in pre-Islamic poetry.

The Prophet (ﷺ) knew well about the existence of these high morals and said in one of his Hadiths:

$$\text{" بُعِثْتُ لِأُتَمِّمَ مَكَارِمَ الْأَخْلَاقِ " (رواه الترمذي)}$$

i.e. "I was sent to complete the high morals" (related by At-Tirmidhi) [18].

The Prophet (ﷺ) had witnessed in his youth in pre-Islamic days a treaty held in the house of Abdulla bin Jad'an between several leaders of Quraish undertaking to help anyone including absolute strangers and visitors who were subjected to injustice until they regain their rights. He said that if he was called to participate in such a treaty after the advent of Islam he would agree.

The Arabs of the Peninsula, with Quraish at their forefront opposed the Prophet (ﷺ) and the message vehmently, but once they accepted Islam they became the hard core of the dawa i.e. the call and invitation of people to the new religion, which reached the various parts of the known world from Spain to the western part of China in the East in a phenomenally short period of around one century. Islam tried to eradicate the negative characters of the pre-Islamic Arabs but built on their positive characteristics such as bravery, chivalry and hospitality, and they gave selflessly to spread Islam. One notices even today the love with which some Muslims in the Far-east receive Arabs especially from the Arabian Peninsula, in appreciation of the sacrifices of their forebearers in spreading Islam. Much of the spread of Islam, especially to the Far-East was through good example of high moral behavior of Arab traders, mainly from the Hadramaut, Yemen.

The Arabs of the inner part of Peninsula at the time of the revealing of the Quran were living in a desert with few permanent constructions and physical edifices of civilization. Their main and almost only art was poetry which they had developed to great heights and had well-known *sawqs* (i.e. markets), like Sawk Ukaz, where their poets met and recited their poems in a competitive spirit. Their greatest poems, such as the famous seven (or ten) odes called Mu'alaqat, had the honour of being hung in the K'aba. The nature of the open desert lent itself to an atmosphere of poetry full of meditation and self-expression and description. The Arabs were very proud of their poetry. This can be easily seen in the writing of the great Arab writer Al-Jahez (159-255 Hijri) in his book Al-Hayawan about poetry and translation of poetry in which he says that poetry is limited to the Arabs and those speaking Arabic. In fact when the Arabs, beginning in the 8th century A.D., translated the knowledge of earlier civilizations such as those of the Greeks, Persians and Indians, etc. including mathematics, astronomy, medicine, etc. they however ignored poetry (such as the Iliad) because they were so proud of their own (incomparable) poetry, and perhaps also because the poetry of these earlier civilizations spoke about the many gods, which contradicted their unitarian faith.

Therefore, the Quran with its miraculously eloquent Arabic, challenged the Arabs in their greatest art and expertise. Miracles of previous prophets challenged the people to whom they were sent in their fields of expertise. Moses (PBUH) performed miracles, by the will of Allah, using his staff or rod which convinced the great magicians who had challenged him of his prophet-hood. This was at a time when the ancient Egyptians were experts in magic. Similarly, the medical miracles of Jesus (PBUH), by the will of Allah, convinced many people at his time of his prophet-hood, taking into account that they were comparatively advanced in medicine. But whereas the miracles of other prophets were effective at the time of those miracles, the Quran remains the Eternal Miracle till the end of time. The Quran says:

$$إِنَّا نَحْنُ نَزَّلْنَا الذِّكْرَ وَإِنَّا لَهُ لَحَافِظُونَ ۝$$

(الحجر/9)

"Indeed, it is We who sent down the Qur'an and indeed, We will assuredly guard it (from corruption)".

Surat Al Hijir, Ayah 9 [19].

The unbelievers accused the Prophet (ﷺ) of being a poet, a priest, a magician, a madman, and so on. They also claimed that they could produce something like the Quran. The Quran defied them and said that if all human beings plus all the Jins tried together to produce something like the Quran they would surely fail to do so. As Quraish failed to do so, the challenge was reduced to the production of just ten suras. As the Arabs failed to do so, the challenge was again reduced to the production of just one sura without defining its length. But they could not produce even one like the shortest sura with only three verses:

$$قُل لَّئِنِ اجْتَمَعَتِ الإِنسُ وَالْجِنُّ عَلَى أَن يَأْتُوا بِمِثْلِ هَٰذَا الْقُرْءَانِ$$
$$لَا يَأْتُونَ بِمِثْلِهِ وَلَوْ كَانَ بَعْضُهُمْ لِبَعْضٍ ظَهِيرًا ۝$$

(الإسراء/88)

[Say: "Surely, if humankind and the jinn were to come together to produce the like of this qur'an, they will never be able to produce

33

the like of it, even if they backed one another with help and support"].

Surat Al-Isra (The Asssensation), Ayah 88. [20]

أَمْ يَقُولُونَ ٱفْتَرَىٰهُ قُلْ فَأْتُواْ بِعَشْرِ سُوَرٍ مِّثْلِهِۦ مُفْتَرَيَٰتٍ وَٱدْعُواْ مَنِ ٱسْتَطَعْتُم مِّن دُونِ ٱللَّهِ إِن كُنتُمْ صَٰدِقِينَ ﴿١٣﴾

(هود/13)

[Or do they say, "He has forged it?" Say: "Then bring you ten Suras the like of it, forged; and call upon whom you are able apart from Allah, if you speak truly"].

Surat Hud, Ayah 13 [21].

أَمْ يَقُولُونَ ٱفْتَرَىٰهُ قُلْ فَأْتُواْ بِسُورَةٍ مِّثْلِهِۦ وَٱدْعُواْ مَنِ ٱسْتَطَعْتُم مِّن دُونِ ٱللَّهِ إِن كُنتُمْ صَٰدِقِينَ ﴿٣٨﴾

(يونس/38)

["Or do they say, "Why he has forged it?" Say: "Then produce a Surah like it; and call on whom you can, apart from Allah, if you speak truly"].

Surat Jonah (Yunis), Ayah 38 [22]

The Quran is a linguistic miracle and several great scholars, for instance Al-Baqalani, have written about this aspect since the early centuries of Islam. But there are several other miraculous aspects related to the Quran.

The fact that it remains the same text as was revealed more than 1400 years ago is in itself a miracle, and it is in the very same words as it was revealed. Muslims believe that other previous scriptures of People of the Book have been subjected to various changes and corruptions in actual words and meanings. The Quran states:

فَوَيْلٌ لِّلَّذِينَ يَكْتُبُونَ ٱلْكِتَٰبَ بِأَيْدِيهِمْ ثُمَّ يَقُولُونَ هَٰذَا مِنْ عِندِ ٱللَّهِ لِيَشْتَرُوا۟ بِهِۦ ثَمَنًا قَلِيلًا ۖ فَوَيْلٌ لَّهُم مِّمَّا كَتَبَتْ أَيْدِيهِمْ وَوَيْلٌ لَّهُم مِّمَّا يَكْسِبُونَ ﴿٧٩﴾

(البقرة/79)

"So woe to those who write the "scripture" with their own hands, then say, "This is from Allah," in order to exchange it for a small price. Woe to them for what their hands have written and woe to them for what they earn."

Surat Al Baqarah (The Cow), Ayah 79 [23].

But the Quran was also a miracle to non-Arabs. The earliest Muslim companions of the Prophet (ﷺ) were not all Arabs for they included persons such as Bilal the black Abesynian who became the *Muazzen* (i.e caller to the prayers) of the Prophet (ﷺ), and Salman the Persian. Islam does not differentiate between Muslims by race and colour but by piety and righteousness. A hadith of the Prophet (ﷺ) states:

لَا فَضْلَ لِعَرَبِيٍّ عَلَى أَعْجَمِيٍّ وَلَا لِعَجَمِيٍّ عَلَى عَرَبِيٍّ وَلَا لِأَحْمَرَ عَلَى أَسْوَدَ وَلَا أَسْوَدَ عَلَى أَحْمَرَ إِلَّا بِالتَّقْوَى (مسند أحمد)

i.e. *An Arab has no superiority over a non-Arab, nor does a non-Arab have any superiority over an Arab; a red (person) has no superiority over a black nor does a black have any superiority over a red except by piety. (Musnad Ahmed)* [24]. The Quran states:

$$\text{يَـٰٓأَيُّهَا ٱلنَّاسُ إِنَّا خَلَقْنَـٰكُم مِّن ذَكَرٍ وَأُنثَىٰ وَجَعَلْنَـٰكُمْ شُعُوبًا وَقَبَآئِلَ لِتَعَارَفُوٓا۟ إِنَّ أَكْرَمَكُمْ عِندَ ٱللَّهِ أَتْقَىٰكُمْ إِنَّ ٱللَّهَ عَلِيمٌ خَبِيرٌ ١٣}$$

(الحجرات/13)

"O mankind, indeed We have created you from a male and a female and made you nations and tribes that you may know one another. Indeed, the most noble of you in the sight of Allah is the most righteous of you. Indeed, Allah is Knowing and Acquainted".
Surat Al Hujurat, Ayah 13. [25]

Another miraculous aspect of the Quran is the fact that it is memorized by millions of Muslims around the World. In fact, the majority of those are not Arabs, and millions of them hardly understand any Arabic.

The Quran, which was revealed fourteen centuries ago, mentioned facts only recently discovered or proven by scientists. This proves without doubt that the Quran must be the literal word of Allah, revealed by Him to the Prophet (ﷺ). Some contemporary medical and scientific discoveries seem to explain statements in the Quran previously not fully interpreted. In fact there is not a single statement in the Quran which can be proved scientifically wrong. The Quran states:

$$\text{سَنُرِيهِمْ ءَايَـٰتِنَا فِى ٱلْءَافَاقِ وَفِىٓ أَنفُسِهِمْ حَتَّىٰ يَتَبَيَّنَ لَهُمْ أَنَّهُ ٱلْحَقُّ أَوَلَمْ يَكْفِ بِرَبِّكَ أَنَّهُ عَلَىٰ كُلِّ شَىْءٍ شَهِيدٌ ٥٣}$$

(فصلت/53)

"We will show them Our signs in the horizons and within themselves until it becomes clear to them that it is the truth. But is it not sufficient concerning your Lord that He is, over all things, a Witness?"
Surat Fusilat, Ayah 53. [26].

36

Introduction

Many prominent scientists from the west and other parts of the World sometimes announce their embracing of Islam at conferences on the scientific miracles in the Holy Quran. A couple of examples include the Thai medical professor Dr. Tejatat Tejasen and the renowned French surgeon Dr. Maurice Bucaille.

The order of the suras of the Quran and of the ayas within them has been ordained by Allah, and the Prophet (ﷺ) always instructed his *sahaba* (i.e. his companions) where to place each aya whenever he received new revelations. Some translators of the meanings of the Quran have taken the liberty to rearrange this order claiming that they followed the chronological order of revelation. This is absolutely unacceptable from the point of view of Islam, and such translations are misleading.

Copies of the Holy Quran produced today are normally in Arabic calligraphy and follow what is called the *Othmani* script. This is in reference to the third rightly guided orthodox Caliph Othman bin Affan (MABPWH) (47 before Hijra-35 Hijri, 576-656 A.D.). He formed a committee to unify the way the Quran was to be written to avoid variance in writing and reading. He advised the committee that whenever there were more ways than one of writing or pronouncing a word to follow the way Quraish did since the Quran was revealed according to the Arabic of Quraish. Later scholars developed the other classically recognized readings of which the seven (or some say up to ten) readings are the most established ones. The seven established readings are referred to seven famous reciters all of whom passed away in the second century Hijri.

Othman (MABPWH) asked Hafsa (MABPWH), one of the widows of the Prophet (ﷺ) and a daughter of Omar bin Al-Khattab the second rightly guided orthodox Caliph (MABPWH), to lend him the only full and correctly arranged master copy of the Quran, originally collected by Abu Bakr As-Siddiq, the first rightly guided orthodox Caliph (MABPWH). It is said that Hafsa (MABPWH), was a literate woman. The master copy was eventually returned to her. The committee of four included Zaid bin Al-Hareth (MABPWH) who had been involved in the compilation of the original master copy, produced several copies, (four to nine copies according to different narrators), and these were sent to different major locations within the Islamic World (such as Kufa, Basra and Damascus) where copies were eventually made from those copies. One copy was retained personally by Othman himself (MABPWH), and it was in his lap when he was assasinated, and drops of his blood fell on some of its pages.

The Othmani script used in the Quran copies today, varies in some ways from today's spelling of standard Arabic, but there was agreement among Muslims to retain the original spelling as far as the Quran itself was concerned, although to make it easier to read and avoid incorrect pronunciation, dots and short vowel signs were added to the true Othmani script after the spread of Islam amongst non-Arabs. It was Abu Al-Aswad Ad-Duali who started the placing of short vowel signs and dots at the instruction of Ali bin Abi-Taleb (MABPWH) who was the fourth rightly guided orthodox Caliph and the cousin of the Prophet Muhammed (صلى الله عليه وسلم). At the time of producing those copies Arabs could read without the need of dots and short vowel signs.

The name Quran is derived from the verb *qara'a*, which means read or recite. Thus the Quran is called so due to the significant amount of reading and recitation which takes place using the Quran. It is recited in formal mandatory and non-mandatory prayers (*salat*), in recitation outside prayers, in dua'a (i.e. supplication and invocation addressed directly to Allah audibly or silently). The Quran is also quoted widely in religious speeches, literary writing, normal conversation, etc.

The Quran has many other names as well, including:

(1) *Al-Kitab, i.e. the Book;*
(2) *Al-Furooqan, i.e. the Criterion (That which distinguishes between truth and falsehood and differentiates right from wrong);*

(3) *Al Mushaf, from the word safha which means page and therefore mushaf is a book whose pages are turned frequently in recitation/reading;*

(4) *Al Dhikir Al Hakeem, i.e. the Wise Remembrance;*

(5) *Al-Huda, i.e. the Guidance;*

(6) *Al-Hikmah, i.e. the wisdom;*

(7) *At-Tanzil, i.e. that which was sent down at intervals;*

(8) *Al-Wahy, i.e. the Revelation;*

(9) *Umm Al-Kitab, i.e. the Mother Book or the Mother of all books.*

The Quran was revealed in Arabic in the dialect of Quraish. All previous messages revealed by Allah to the various prophets were revealed in the languages of their people. The Quran states:

$$وَمَآ أَرْسَلْنَا مِن رَّسُولٍ إِلَّا بِلِسَانِ قَوْمِهِۦ لِيُبَيِّنَ لَهُمْ$$

$$فَيُضِلُّ ٱللَّهُ مَن يَشَآءُ وَيَهْدِى مَن يَشَآءُ وَهُوَ ٱلْعَزِيزُ$$

$$ٱلْحَكِيمُ ٤$$

(إبراهيم/4)

"And We did not send any messenger except [speaking] in the language of his people to state clearly for them, and Allah sends astray [thereby] whom He wills and guides whom He wills. And He is the Exalted in Might, the Wise."

Surat Ibrahim, Ayah 4 [27].

It was obvious that the Quran had to be revealed in Arabic because that was the language understood and spoken by Muhammad (ﷺ) and it was the language of his people.

But the previous messages were mainly confined to the people to whom they were sent, whereas the Quran was meant as a message to all of humanity as mentioned earlier in verse Surat Saba, Aya 28. Of course the onus was upon the Arabs to whom it was first sent to absorb the message and believe in it fully, enact its teachings as stewards, then convey it to other nations through translation and good example. But if fought to cease from delivering the message, it was their right to defend themselves and it was their duty to continue to deliver the message.

After the Treaty of Hudaybiyah with Quraish in the 6th Hijri year (628 A.D.), the Prophet (ﷺ) sent messages to nine kings and rulers. These were the Christian Byzantine emperor, Heraclitus, the Persian emperor, the Christian ruler of Egypt Al-Muqauqas, the Christian Negus of Abyssinia (who was different from the Negus who had welcomed the early Muslims who sought refuge in his country from the torture or harassment of Quraish), the Jacobite Al-Hareth Al-Ghassani in the Levant, and other rulers in Bahrain, Yamama, Oman, and Yemen. In his message to Christian rulers he included a verse from the Quran that says:

قُلْ يَٰأَهْلَ ٱلْكِتَٰبِ تَعَالَوْا۟ إِلَىٰ كَلِمَةٍ سَوَآءٍ بَيْنَنَا وَبَيْنَكُمْ أَلَّا نَعْبُدَ إِلَّا ٱللَّهَ وَلَا نُشْرِكَ بِهِۦ شَيْـًٔا وَلَا يَتَّخِذَ بَعْضُنَا بَعْضًا أَرْبَابًا مِّن دُونِ ٱللَّهِ فَإِن تَوَلَّوْا۟ فَقُولُوا۟ ٱشْهَدُوا۟ بِأَنَّا مُسْلِمُونَ ﴿٦٤﴾

(آل عمران/64)

"Say, "O People of the Scripture, come to a word that is equitable between us and you - that we will not worship except Allah and not associate any other partners with Him and not take one another as lords (i.e. erect from among ourselves, lords) instead of Allah." But if they turn away, then say, "Bear witness that we are Muslims [submitting to Him].""

Surat Aal-Imran, Ayah 64 [28]

Introduction

The poetry of the Arabs before Islam was an advanced art, but the Quran was a linguistic miracle that challenged them. Arabic is a very rich mature old language that was capable of conveying the Quran. The Arabic language is several thousand years old and its words have about 16000 linguistic roots, This is far more than the linguistic roots of other languages such as Hebrew, Greek or Latin. Arabic has the characteristic that makes it possible to create a large family of words from a root. If one compares the English of the Middle Ages with the English of Elizabethan times and of modern times one would see major differences. Arabic, however, has remained more or less the same from pre-Islamic times until today. Of course, the Quran with its richness and beauty has played a major role in keeping the language very much alive and fresh throughout the past fourteen centuries. The Quran says:

(يوسف/2)

"Indeed, We have sent it down as an Arabic Qur'an that you might understand."

Surat Yusuf (Prophet Joseph), Ayah 2 [29]

وَلَوْ جَعَلْنَٰهُ قُرْءَانًا أَعْجَمِيًّا لَّقَالُوا لَوْلَا فُصِّلَتْ ءَايَٰتُهُۥٓ ءَأَعْجَمِيٌّ وَعَرَبِيٌّ قُلْ هُوَ لِلَّذِينَ ءَامَنُوا هُدًى وَشِفَآءٌ وَٱلَّذِينَ لَا يُؤْمِنُونَ فِىٓ ءَاذَانِهِمْ وَقْرٌ وَهُوَ عَلَيْهِمْ عَمًى أُوْلَٰٓئِكَ يُنَادَوْنَ مِن مَّكَانٍ بَعِيدٍ ٤٤

(فصلت/44)

"And if We had made it a non-Arabic Qur'an, they would have said, "Why are its verses not explained in detail [in our language]? Is

it a foreign [recitation] and an Arab [messenger]?" Say, "It is, for those who believe; a guidance and cure." And those who do not believe - in their ears is deafness, and it is upon them blindness. They are (like people who are being) called from too far (a distant place)."

Surat Fusillat, Ayah 44 [30].

It is said that Arabic was the language used by several older prophets mentioned in the Holy Quran such as Saleh (PBUH), Hud (PBUH), Shuaib (PBUH) and Ismail (Ishmael) (PBUH). Arabic was the language of science throughout the world during the Middle-Ages, and is today one of the six United Nations official main languages. Its richness has served the Quran well, but the Quran is largely what has given it its eminence in the world.

Chapter 1

Legitimacy of the Translation of the Holy Quran

Muslims believe that the actual words of the Quran are divine words of Allah, revealed to Prophet Muhammad (ﷺ) by Archangel Gabriel and are, therefore, untranslatable literally. Any translation of the words of the Quran will not be equivalent to the Quran, and in the opinion of most Muslim scholars, could not be considered holy like the Quran itself. For instance according to Muslim scholars the Quran in its Arabic script should not be handled by Muslims in a state of major ritual impurity (e.g. during the menstruation cycle), but according to Muslim scholars, this does not apply to a translation of the meanings of the Quran.

Muslim scholars agree that a literal translation of the text of the Quran is not achievable, and according to most of them is not permissible. In any case such a translation could be misleading. For instance, let us look at the following aya:

$$\text{وَلَا تَجْعَلْ يَدَكَ مَغْلُولَةً إِلَىٰ عُنُقِكَ وَلَا تَبْسُطْهَا كُلَّ الْبَسْطِ فَتَقْعُدَ}$$
$$\text{مَلُومًا مَّحْسُورًا ﴿٢٩﴾}$$

(الإسراء/29)

"And do not make your hand [as] chained to your neck or extend it completely and [thereby] become blamed and insolvent."
Surat Al Isra (The Assensation), Ayah 29 [31]

43

A literal translation would say that you should not tie or chain your hand to your neck, nor extend it fully, whereas the true meaning of the *aya* is that you should not be too miserly nor overspend.

The Quran itself states that it is impossible to write anything like the Quran. To a Muslim this is true in Arabic as well as in any other language.

$$قُل لَّئِنِ ٱجْتَمَعَتِ ٱلْإِنسُ وَٱلْجِنُّ عَلَىٰ أَن يَأْتُوا۟ بِمِثْلِ هَٰذَا ٱلْقُرْءَانِ لَا يَأْتُونَ بِمِثْلِهِۦ وَلَوْ كَانَ بَعْضُهُمْ لِبَعْضٍ ظَهِيرًا ٨٨$$

(الإسراء/ 88)

"Say: "Surely, if humankind and the jinn were to come toghther to produce the like of this Qur'an, they will never be able to produce the like of it, though even if they backed one another with help and support."

Surat Al-Isra (The Asssensation), Ayah 88 [32]

However, most scholars say that it is permissible to translate the meanings of the Quran, since such a translation makes it possible for Muslims who do not know Arabic to understand, albeit approximately, what the Quran states. Similarly, it also makes it possible for non-Muslims to form an understanding of the message of the Quran. Islam is a religion that asks its followers to spread the message of Islam, and invite non-Muslims to embrace Islam, and, therefore, reasonably correct translations can help a propagator of the religion in his efforts to teach and explain Islam to non-Arabs.

Chapter 1: Legitimacy of the Translation of the Holy Quran

The Quran says:

$$\text{ٱلَّذِينَ يُبَلِّغُونَ رِسَٰلَٰتِ ٱللَّهِ وَيَخْشَوْنَهُ وَلَا يَخْشَوْنَ أَحَدًا إِلَّا ٱللَّهَ وَكَفَىٰ بِٱللَّهِ حَسِيبًا ۝}$$

(الأحزاب/39)

"(Allah praises) those who convey the messages of Allah and fear Him and do not fear anyone but Allah. And sufficient is Allah to hold all to account".

Surat Al Ahzaab, (The Confederates), Ayah 39. [33]

It also states:

$$\text{ٱدْعُ إِلَىٰ سَبِيلِ رَبِّكَ بِٱلْحِكْمَةِ وَٱلْمَوْعِظَةِ ٱلْحَسَنَةِ وَجَٰدِلْهُم بِٱلَّتِي هِيَ أَحْسَنُ إِنَّ رَبَّكَ هُوَ أَعْلَمُ بِمَن ضَلَّ عَن سَبِيلِهِ وَهُوَ أَعْلَمُ بِٱلْمُهْتَدِينَ ۝}$$

(النحل/125)

"Invite to the way of your Lord with wisdom and good guidance (preaching), and argue with them in a way that is best. Indeed, your Lord is most knowing of who has strayed from His way, and He is most knowing of who is [rightly] guided."

Surat An-Nahl (The Bee), Ayah 125 [34]

The Prophet (ﷺ) said:

"بَلِّغُوا عَنِّي وَلَوْ آيَةً" (رواه البخاري وآخرون)

45

i.e. *"Convey from me even a (single) aya."* (Narrated by Al-Bukhari and others) [35]

Some scholars have argued that a translation of even the meanings of the Quran is not permissible, and yet there are some who have argued that even the tafsir (i.e. interpretation) should not be translated. One of their arguments is that translation of the Quran or its meanings or interpretation was not done in the days of the Prophet (ﷺ) and his companions, nor was that done in the early centuries of Islam, and yet millions of people embraced Islam and recited the Holy Quran always in Arabic. However, this is an extreme view, and is not the common view of contemporary scholars.

According to most Muslim scholars, a Muslim may not call the *Adhan* (i.e. call for prayers) or say his prayers except in Arabic. Only Abu Hanifah (80-150 H, 699-767 A.D.), the head of one of the four major Sunni schools of Islamic Jurisprudence, is said to have opined that Muslims may recite a translation in their prayers. His two companion scholars, Abu Yousuf and Muhammad opined that that was only allowed for those who did not know Arabic. In any case, this particular opinion of Abu Hanifah and his two companions is not relevent today as far as we know.

The Quran itself stresses in several ayas that it is in clear and eloquent Arabic. Here are some of those ayas:

$$\text{إِنَّا جَعَلْنَاهُ قُرْآنًا عَرَبِيًّا لَّعَلَّكُمْ تَعْقِلُونَ ﴿٣﴾}$$

((الزخرف/3))

"Indeed, We have made it an Arabic Qur'an that you might understand." Surat Al Zukhruf, Ayah 3 [36]

$$\text{إِنَّا أَنزَلْنَاهُ قُرْآنًا عَرَبِيًّا لَّعَلَّكُمْ تَعْقِلُونَ ﴿٢﴾}$$

(يوسف/2)

46

"Indeed, We have sent it down as an Arabic Qur'an that you might understand."

Surat Yusuf (Prophet Joseph), Ayah 2 [29/37]

$$\text{قُرْءَانًا عَرَبِيًّا غَيْرَ ذِى عِوَجٍ لَّعَلَّهُمْ يَتَّقُونَ ﴿٢٨﴾}$$

(الزمر/28)

"(It is) an Arabic Qur'an, without any crookedness (deviance) that they might become righteous" Surat Al-Zumar, Ayah 28. [38]

$$\text{كِتَابٌ فُصِّلَتْ ءَايَتُهُ قُرْءَانًا عَرَبِيًّا لِّقَوْمٍ يَعْلَمُونَ ﴿٣﴾}$$

(فصلت/3)

"A Book whose verses have been detailed, an Arabic Qur'an for a people who comprehend"

Surat Fussilat, Ayah 3 [39].

$$\text{وَكَذَلِكَ أَنزَلْنَاهُ حُكْمًا عَرَبِيًّا وَلَئِنِ اتَّبَعْتَ أَهْوَاءَهُم بَعْدَمَا جَاءَكَ مِنَ الْعِلْمِ مَا لَكَ مِنَ اللَّهِ مِن وَلِيٍّ وَلَا وَاقٍ ﴿٣٧﴾}$$

(الرعد/37)

"And thus We have revealed it as an Arabic legislation. And if you should follow their inclinations after what has come to you of knowledge, you would not have against Allah any ally or any protector."

Surat Al-Ra'd, Ayah 37 [40]

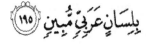

(الشعراء/195)

"In the perspicuous Arabic tongue."
Surat Al Shu'ara, Ayah 195 [41]

The miraculous nature of the Quran is not limited to its eloquence and its use of the language, but also to the fact that none of the statements in the Quran have ever been in contradiction with any newly discovered scientific findings in the fields of astronomy, geology, physics, medicine, etc., which could not have been known to any person in the days of the Prophet (ﷺ) about 14 centuries ago. The only explanation possible is, therefore, that the Quran was a revelation from Allah.

Chapter 2

The Importance of Al-Fatihah

Al-Fatihah (الفاتحة) is the opening *sura* (chapter) of the Noble Qur'an. Al-Fathah has seven verses, and consists of 29 words with a total of 139 letters.

Al-Fatihah was one of the early suras revealed in Makkah, and it was revealed as a complete sura in the present order of its ayas. Some scholars believe that it was revealed in Madinah and some believe that it was revealed twice, once in Makkah and a second time in Madinah. But it was probably revealed in Makkah because of the following two reasons: The first is that prayer was ordained on the Prophet when he was still in Makkah and most likely his prayers started by reading Al-Fatihah. The other reason is that Al-Fatihah is mentioned in Surat Al-Hijr which is a Makkian sura:

وَلَقَدْ ءَاتَيْنَاكَ سَبْعًا مِّنَ ٱلْمَثَانِى وَٱلْقُرْءَانَ ٱلْعَظِيمَ ۝

((الحجر/87

"And indeed, We have bestowed upon you seven of Al-Mathani (seven repeatedly recited verses) and the Grand Qur'an."

Surat Al Hijr, Ayah 87 [42].

According to several well-known authoritative interpreters of the Quran, the seven of Al-Mathani or seven-oft repeated ones is another name of Al-Fatihah, reflecting the fact that the seven verses of Al-Fatihah are the only verses of the Qur'an which must be read in every *rak'a* (i.e.

49

kneeling which in fact denotes the whole sequence of reciting of Quran, kneeling, prostrating, etc.) of every prayer. It is as such also called simply Al-Mathani referring to its repetition in prayer. In fact, one of the names of Al-Fatihah is Suart Al-Salat (سورة الصلاة) i.e. the Sura of Prayer.

The above aya is an interesting testimony; for although Al-Fatihah is part of the Qur'an, Allah *Subhanah Wa-Taala* (SWT) (i.e. glory and exaltation to Him) indicates its special significance by saying *"....seven of Al-Mathani (seven repeatedly recited verses i.e. Surat Al-Fatihah) and the Grand Quran"*. Furthermore, in this aya the seven verses of Al-Fatihah are identified as a great gift from Allah (SWT) in addition to the Glorious Quran.

Al-Fatihah gets its name from the Arabic base-word (verb) *fataha* which means he opened. Al-Fatihah therefore means "The Opening One", i.e. "The Opening Surat". It has several other names beside Al-Fatihah and the Seven-Oft Repeated Ones which reflect its attributes. It is thus called Umm Al-Kitab or "The Mother of the Book", as *umm* i.e. (mother). It is here a word that denotes the origin and starting point, and *kitab* i.e. book refers to the Qur'an. It is also called Umm-Al Qur'an or "The Mother of the Qur'an".

In a *Qudsi* hadith [44] of the Prophet (ﷺ) about Al-Fatihah: On the authority of Abu Hurayrah (may Allah be pleased with him) from the Prophet (ﷺ), who said:

عن أبي هريرة رضي الله عنه عن النبي صلى الله عليه وسلم قال: "من صلى صلاة لم يقرأ فيها بأم القرآن، فهي خداج ثلاثا غير تمام، فقيل لأبي هريرة، إنا نكون وراء الإمام؟ فقال: اقرأ بها في نفسك، فإني سمعت رسول الله صلى الله عليه وسلم يقول: قال الله تعالى: "قسمت الصلاة بيني وبين عبدي نصفين، ولعبدي ما سأل، فإذا قال العبد:

{ الحمد لله رب العالمين }

قال الله تعالى: حمدني عبدي، وإذا قال:

{ الرحمن الرحيم }

قال الله تعالى: أثنى علي عبدي، وإذا قال:

{ مالك يوم الدين }

قال: مجدني عبدي، وقال مرة: فوض إلي عبدي، فإذا قال:

{ إياك نعبد وإياك }

نستعين

قال: هذا بيني وبين عبدي ولعبدي ما سأل، فإذا قال:

اهدنا الصراط المستقيم صراط الذين أنعمت عليهم غير المغضوب
{
عليهم ولا الضالين

قال: هذا لعبدي ولعبدي ما سأل.

(رواه مسلم)

"A prayer performed by someone who has not recited the Essence of the Quran (i.e Al Fathiha, the first Sura of the Quran) during it is deficient (and he repeated the word three times), incomplete. Someone said to Abu Hurayrah: [Even though] we are behind the imam? He said: Recite it to yourself, for I have heard the Prophet (May the blessings and peace of Allah be upon him) say: Allah (mighty and sublime be He, has said: "I have divided prayer between Myself and My servant into two halves, and My servant shall have what he has asked for. When the servant says: Al-hamdu lillahi rabbi 'l'-alamin, Allah (mighty and sublime be He) says: My servant has praised Me. And when he says: Ar-rahmani 'r-rahim, Allah (mighty and sublime be He) says: My servant

has extolled Me, and when he says: Maliki yawmi 'd-din, Allah says: My servant has glorified Me – and on one occasion He said: My servant has submitted to My power. And when he says: Iyyaka na'budu wa iyyaka nasta'in, He says: This is between Me and My servant, and My servant shall have what he has asked for. And when he says: Ihdina's-sirata 'l-mustaqim, sirata 'lladhina an'amta 'alayhim ghayri 'l-maghdubi 'alayhim wa la d-dallin, He says: This is for My servant, and My servant shall have what he has asked for. (This was Narrated by Muslim) [43]

Al-Fatihah is also called Al-Wafiah (الوافية) or "The Complete One" as it cannot be split, or part read in prayer but must be read as a whole. Interestingly, it is also called Al-Kafia (الكافية) or "The One that Suffices" because it carries and provides the essence of the words of the Lord (SWT) i.e. the whole of the Qur'an.

In that respect, the Prophet Muhammad (ﷺ) said *"Umm Al Kita'ab suffices others but no other will suffice in its place!"* [44]

أم الكتاب عوض من غيرها وليس غيرها منها عوض

It has also been referred to as Al-Shafiya (الشافية) i.e. "The Curing One" and Al-Shifa i.e. "The Cure", most probably because it was used in conjunction with "Prophetic Medicine" for the purpose of curing the sick.

عن عبد الملك بن عمير قال: قال رسول الله صلى الله عليه وسلم في فاتحة الكتاب شفاء من كل داء (سنن الدارمي)

Abdul-Malik bin Umair related that the Prophet (ﷺ) said *"In the Opening of the Book there is cure from all illnesses"* (Related in Sunan Ad-Darimi). [45]

إذا وضعت جنبك على الفراش وقرأت فاتحة الكتاب وقل هو الله أحد فقد أمنت من كل شيء إلا الموت.

Chapter 2: The Importance of Al-Fatihah

And in another Hadith the Prophet (ﷺ) said: "If you place your self on your bed, and you read the Al fathiah of the Book and the Sura "say Allah is One, by it you would have secured yourself from everything except death" [46]

Also in his book "The Prophetic Medicine", Ibn Al Qayyim Al Jawziyya states: *"In general, the contents of the Fatiha, which are: the sincerity of the adoration, the laudation of Allah, the entrust of one's soul to him, the imploration of His whole graces that are: the guidance that brings favors and repulses the spite – all these elements constitute one of the most beneficial healing remedies."* [47]

Moreover, Al-Fatihah has also been called Al-Ruqiya (الراقية) or "The Protecting One"; and Al-Waqiyah(الواقية) or the "Preventive or Protective One" as it protects its reader from harm" [48]

Other names include Al-Kanz (الكنز)i.e. the Treasure; Al-Asas (الأساس) i.e. the Foundation; Al-Noor (النور) i.e. the Light; Surat Al-Hamd (سورة الحمد) i.e. the Sura of Praise; The Sura of Taleem Al-Mas'alah(سورة تعليم المسألة) i.e. the Sura of teaching of the meaning (of existence); Surat Al-Munajat (سورة المناجاة)i.e. The Sura of Soliloquy (between man and the Creator) as well as Surat Al-Tafweed (سورة التفويض)which means the Sura of Delegacy. Some writers have noted that Al-Fatihah has in excess of 20 names, and this is possible as it possesses such a multitude of integrated concepts, aspects and immense depth of meaning [49]

Interestingly, and most importantly Al-Fatihah is a dialogue and a protocol of approach of mankind to the Creator, the Sustainer and the True Guide. Al-Fatihah is about the Truth and about how mankind approaches Allah (SWT), first by reading in His Name, then by being grateful to Him whilst recognizing His mastery over absolutely everything in All Worlds, recognizing His greatest attributes, also realizing that He is the Master of the Day of Reckoning, then confessing to Him (and Him alone) that it is to Him one prays and to Him (and Him alone) does one ask for ultimate support and then ask after this that He may show one the way to the straight and right path, the path of the righteous and not the path of the unrighteous and ultimately doomed.

In his book *"The Opening Chapter of the Qur'an"*, Mawlana Abul Kalam Azad expresses:

"God is here invoked in His attributes, the manifestations of which man beholds day-in day-out, however much he may, through in-difference, neglect to reflect over them. Here you have man's admission of his absolute dependence on God, his acknowledgement of the divine kindness shown to him, his earnest yearning to be saved from the pitfalls of life and to be led along the straight path." [50]

Abdul Basit noted in his book "the Essence of the Qur'an": *"In fact these seven verses form a complete unit by themselves. This beautiful chapter is so thorough, comprehensive, and universal that in brief it contains basic teachings of the Glorious Qur'an. Many Western scholars, even Christian missionary workers, have been profoundly impressed by the universal characteristic and sublime style of prayer. The followers of the monotheistic religions; whether Jews or Christians, could all recite Sura Al-Fatihah without any reservation. It is this universal aspect of the Lord's prayer that has attracted the attention of many non-Muslim scholars".* [51]

He goes on to quote Alfred Guillaume, a noted orientalist remarking: *"There is nothing in the official worship of Islam in which a Christian could not join, and one who understands the word of praise and adoration is tempted to do so".*

Finally, this chapter can be considered only a brief introduction to Al-Fatihah and in these further chapters we hope to be able to elaborate further on the interpretation of the seven wonderful ayas.

Chapter 3

الاستعاذة

Al-Istiadah or Seeking Refuge

The Quran states:

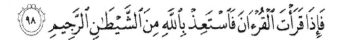

(النحل/98)

"So when you read the Qur'an, [first] seek refuge in Allah from Satan, the expelled one [from His mercy]".
Surat An Nahl (The Bee), Ayah 98. [52]

Thus a Muslim is required to say before reading the Quran, including Al- Fatihah or any chapters or verses of the Quran:

"أعوذ بالله من الشيطان الرجيم"

i.e. "I take refuge in Allah from the accursed Satan". This is to prepare oneself to receive the words of Allah with a clear mind, with no distractions by Satan or the Devil.

In Islam the devil or *shaytan* شيطان, plural: شياطين *shayaṭeen*) is known as *Iblees* or *Iblis* (Arabic: إبليس, plural: أبالسة *abalisah*). In Islam *Iblees* is from the Jinn and is not a fallen angel as in Christianity. Iblees refused to bow to Adam when Allah created Adam and instructed the angels to bow to him.

The Quran states:

$$
\text{وَإِذْ قُلْنَا لِلْمَلَٰٓئِكَةِ ٱسْجُدُواْ لِءَادَمَ فَسَجَدُوٓاْ إِلَّآ إِبْلِيسَ كَانَ مِنَ ٱلْجِنِّ}
$$

$$
\text{فَفَسَقَ عَنْ أَمْرِ رَبِّهِۦٓ أَفَتَتَّخِذُونَهُۥ وَذُرِّيَّتَهُۥٓ أَوْلِيَآءَ مِن دُونِى وَهُمْ}
$$

$$
\text{لَكُمْ عَدُوٌّۢ بِئْسَ لِلظَّٰلِمِينَ بَدَلًا ﴿٥٠﴾}
$$

(الكهف/50)

"And when We said to the angels, "Prostrate to Adam," and they prostrated, except for Iblees. He was of the jinn and departed from the command of his Lord. Then will you take him and his descendants as allies other than Me while they are enemies to you? Wretched it is for the wrongdoers as an exchange."

Surat Al Kahf (The Cave), 50 [53]

It is worthy to note that there are several other Ayat (Verses) in the Quran that discuss this dialogue between Allah (SWT) and Satan when he was ordered to prostrate to Allah's creation and he chose to disobay his Creater. These include Surat Al Baqarah (The Cow), Ayah 34 and so on.

Iblees committed the great sin of disobeying Allah. He also committed the great sin of arrogance by thinking himself better than Adam because he was created from fire whilst Adam was created from clay. The Quran states:

$$
\text{قَالَ أَنَا۠ خَيْرٌ مِّنْهُ خَلَقْتَنِى مِن نَّارٍ وَخَلَقْتَهُۥ مِن طِينٍ ﴿٧٦﴾}
$$

(ص/76)

"He (Iblis) said, "I am better than him. You created me from fire and created him from clay.""

Surat Sad, Ayah 76 [54]

56

Chapter 3: Al-Istiadah or Seeking Refuge

The Prophet (ﷺ) said:

لاَ يَدْخُلُ الْجَنَّةَ مَنْ كَانَ فِي قَلْبِهِ مِثْقَالُ حَبَّةٍ مِنْ خَرْدَلٍ مِنْ كِبْرٍ وَلاَ يَدْخُلُ النَّارَ مَنْ كَانَ فِي قَلْبِهِ مِثْقَالُ حَبَّةٍ مِنْ خَرْدَلٍ مِنْ إِيمَانٍ

i.e. *"No one will enter Paradise who has even a mustard-seed's weight of arrogance in his heart, and no one will enter Hell who has even a mustard-seed's weight of faith in his heart"*. (Sunan Ibn Majah) [55]

And another Hadith also it states:

"لا يدخل الجنة من كان في قلبه مثقال ذرة من كبر. قال رجل: إن الرجل يحب أن يكون ثوبه حسناً، ونعله حسنة، قال: إن الله جميل يحب الجمال، الكبر بطر الحق، وغمط الناس". (رواه مسلم، الترمذي، أبو داوود، ابن ماجه وأحمد).

"He who has in his heart the weight of a mustard seed of pride shall not enter Paradise. A person (amongst his hearers) said: Verily a person loves that his dress should be fine, and his shoes should be fine. He (the Holy Prophet) remarked: Verily, Allah is Graceful and He loves Grace. Pride is disdaining the truth (out of self-conceit) and contempt for the people." (Narrated by Muslim, At-Tirmidhi, Abu Daood, Ibn Majah, and Ahmed) [56]

Because Iblees refused the orders of Allah to bow to Adam he was banished from the mercy of Allah forever, and deserved to be permanently placed in Hell at the Day of Reckoning. Adam and Eve also disobeyed Allah by eating from the forbidden tree, but they admitted their guilt and weakness and asked for forgiveness. Allah removed them from Paradise and transferred them to our Earth to strive with their offspring to deserve Paradise, through living righteously. This is stated in the Quran in Surat Al-Baqara 35-39 as follows:

وَقُلْنَا يَـٰٓـَٔادَمُ ٱسْكُنْ أَنتَ وَزَوْجُكَ ٱلْجَنَّةَ وَكُلَا مِنْهَا رَغَدًا حَيْثُ شِئْتُمَا وَلَا تَقْرَبَا هَـٰذِهِ ٱلشَّجَرَةَ فَتَكُونَا مِنَ ٱلظَّـٰلِمِينَ ﴿٣٥﴾

[And We said, "O Adam, dwell, you and your wife, in Paradise and eat therefrom in [ease and] abundance from wherever you will. But do not approach this tree, lest you be among the wrongdoers."]

فَأَزَلَّهُمَا ٱلشَّيْطَـٰنُ عَنْهَا فَأَخْرَجَهُمَا مِمَّا كَانَا فِيهِ وَقُلْنَا ٱهْبِطُوا۟ بَعْضُكُمْ لِبَعْضٍ عَدُوٌّ وَلَكُمْ فِى ٱلْأَرْضِ مُسْتَقَرٌّ وَمَتَـٰعٌ إِلَىٰ حِينٍ ﴿٣٦﴾

"But Satan caused them to slip out of it and removed them from that (condition) in which they had been. And We said, "Go down, [all of you], as enemies to one another, and you will have upon the earth a place of settlement and provision for a time."

فَتَلَقَّىٰٓ ءَادَمُ مِن رَّبِّهِۦ كَلِمَـٰتٍ فَتَابَ عَلَيْهِ إِنَّهُۥ هُوَ ٱلتَّوَّابُ ٱلرَّحِيمُ ﴿٣٧﴾

"Then Adam received from his Lord (some) words, and He accepted his repentance. Indeed, it is He Who is the Accepting of repentance, the Most Merciful."

قُلْنَا ٱهْبِطُوا۟ مِنْهَا جَمِيعًا فَإِمَّا يَأْتِيَنَّكُم مِّنِّى هُدًى فَمَن تَبِعَ هُدَاىَ فَلَا خَوْفٌ عَلَيْهِمْ وَلَا هُمْ يَحْزَنُونَ ﴿٣٨﴾

"We said, "Go down from it, all of you. And when guidance comes to you from Me, whoever follows My guidance - there will be no fear concerning them, nor will they grieve."

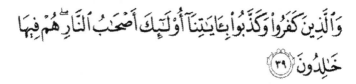

وَٱلَّذِينَ كَفَرُوا۟ وَكَذَّبُوا۟ بِـَٔايَٰتِنَآ أُو۟لَٰٓئِكَ أَصْحَٰبُ ٱلنَّارِ هُمْ فِيهَا خَٰلِدُونَ ﴿٣٩﴾

(البقرة/ 35-39)

"And those who disbelieve and deny Our signs - those will be companions (dwellers) of the (Hell) Fire; they will abide therein eternally."

Surat Al Baqarah Ayah 35-39 [57].

Asking for refuge in Allah from the shaytan is mentioned in several verses of the Quran. The imperative verb فَٱسْتَعِذْ (so ask for refuge) is in 4 ayas namely Al-Aaraf Ayah 200, An-Nahl Ayah 98, Ghafer Ayah 56 and Fussilat Ayah 36. The verb أعوذ (I take refuge) is mentioned in 7 ayas namely in the following Suras: Al-Baqarah Ayah 67; Hud Ayah 47; Mariam Ayah 18; Al-Mu'minoon Ayah 97 and Ayah 98; Al-Falaq Ayah 1; and An-Nas Ayah 1.

The plural word shayateen is mentioned 13 times in the Quran. Iblees is mentioned in 11 verses.

The worst enemy of human beings is Iblees. He has a grudge against Adam and his offspring. He wishes to drag them to hellfire together with him. He asked Allah to allow him to tempt them to do evil deeds to deserve to go to hell. Whilst angels and all creatures, other than human beings and jinn, merely do what Allah has ordained them to do. Human beings and jinn are creatures who have been given by a choice of their actions by Allah and, therefore, are accountable.

The Quran states:

قَالَ أَنظِرْنِىٓ إِلَىٰ يَوْمِ يُبْعَثُونَ ﴿١٤﴾

قَالَ إِنَّكَ مِنَ ٱلْمُنظَرِينَ ﴿١٥﴾

قَالَ فَبِمَآ أَغْوَيْتَنِي لَأَقْعُدَنَّ لَهُمْ صِرَٰطَكَ ٱلْمُسْتَقِيمَ ﴿١٦﴾

ثُمَّ لَآتِيَنَّهُم مِّنۢ بَيْنِ أَيْدِيهِمْ وَمِنْ خَلْفِهِمْ وَعَنْ أَيْمَٰنِهِمْ وَعَن شَمَآئِلِهِمْ وَلَا تَجِدُ أَكْثَرَهُمْ شَٰكِرِينَ ﴿١٧﴾

(الأعراف / 14-17)

"(Satan) said, "Reprieve me until the Day they are resurrected."
"(Allah) said, "Indeed, you are of those reprieved."
"(Satan) said, "Because You have allowed me to go astray I will surely sit in wait for them on Your straight path (to lure them from it)."
"Then I will come to them from before them and from behind them and on their right and on their left, and You will not find most of them grateful (to You)".

Surat Al A'raf, Ayah 14-17. [58].

But Iblees has no power other than the power to cast evil suggestions into the chests of human beings, which is something like whispering, and although the Quran does mention appointing jinn to assist those who are far from Allah in a general context. The Quran states:

يَٰبَنِىٓ ءَادَمَ لَا يَفْتِنَنَّكُمُ ٱلشَّيْطَٰنُ كَمَآ أَخْرَجَ أَبَوَيْكُم مِّنَ ٱلْجَنَّةِ يَنزِعُ عَنْهُمَا لِبَاسَهُمَا لِيُرِيَهُمَا سَوْءَٰتِهِمَآ إِنَّهُۥ يَرَىٰكُمْ هُوَ وَقَبِيلُهُۥ مِنْ حَيْثُ لَا تَرَوْنَهُمْ إِنَّا جَعَلْنَا ٱلشَّيَٰطِينَ أَوْلِيَآءَ لِلَّذِينَ لَا يُؤْمِنُونَ ﴿٢٧﴾

(الأعراف/27)

60

"O children of Adam, let not Satan tempt you as he removed your parents from Paradise, stripping them of their clothing to show them their private parts. Indeed, he sees you, he and his tribe, from where you do not see them. Indeed, We have made the devils allies to those who do not believe."

Surat Al A'raf, Ayah 27. [59].

Iblees focuses his efforts of temptation and seduction on persons who are trying to do righteous deeds, as those who are doing evil deeds are already on the wrong path. Reading the Quran is one of the best deeds a human being can do and, therefore, Iblees tries to distract the reader. But saying the *istiadah* helps the reader to absorb the verses with a clear and spiritually receptive mind.

Iblees is, in fact, at the center of all the struggles of human beings between good and evil, and between right and wrong throughout life in this world.

بِسْمِ اللهِ الرَّحْمٰنِ الرَّحِيمِ ۞ الْحَمْدُ لِلّٰهِ رَبِّ الْعَالَمِينَ ۞ الرَّحْمٰنِ الرَّحِيمِ ۞ مَالِكِ يَوْمِ الدِّينِ ۞ إِيَّاكَ نَعْبُدُ وَإِيَّاكَ نَسْتَعِينُ ۞ اهْدِنَا الصِّرَاطَ الْمُسْتَقِيمَ ۞ صِرَاطَ الَّذِينَ أَنْعَمْتَ عَلَيْهِمْ غَيْرِ الْمَغْضُوبِ عَلَيْهِمْ وَلَا الضَّالِّينَ ۞

Chapter 4

البَسْمَلَة: بِسْمِ اللَّهِ الرَّحْمَٰنِ الرَّحِيمِ

Al-Basmalah:
Bismillahi Ar-Rahman Ar-Raheem

The first sentence of the Quran, and therefore, also of *Al-Fatihah* or The Opening is بسم الله الرحمن الرحيم *pronounced Bismillahi Ar-Rahman Ar-Raheem*, meaning *"In the name of Allah The "Rahman" the Most Merciful"*. The above sentence is known as the *Basmalah*. It is the first *aya* (or verse) of the Opening, or in other words the first of the Seven Oft-Repeated-Ones.

The Basmalah appears 114 times in the Quran. It appears at the beginning of 113 of the 114 suras of the Quran. The one exception is the beginning of Surat *At-Taubah* (i.e. Repentance), also called *Baraat* (i.e. Immunity) as the Prophet (ﷺ) did not mention the Basmalah when he recited it to his followers/companions. The Basmalah also appears as part of aya 30 of Surat *An-Naml* (i.e. Ants):

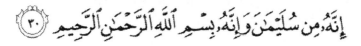

(النمل/30)

"Verily, it is from Sulaiman (Solomon), and verily it (reads): In the Name of Allah, the Most Gracious, the Most Merciful.".
Surat Al Naml (The Ants), Ayah 30 [60].

Although there is agreement that the Basmalah is part of the the above aya and, therefore, part of the Quran, there are, however, three opinions amongst scholars regarding the Basmalah at the beginning of the suras [61]:

1) That it is an aya in Al-Fatihah and all the other 112 suras which start with the Basmalah;
2) That it is an independent aya revealed for separating suras and as a blessing;
3) That it is an aya in Al-Fatihah but not in all other 112 suras;

There is also a forth permutation that it is neither an aya in Al-Fatihah, nor at the beginning of any other sura. But this is not a strong opinion and no refrences have been found supporting this.

Sunni Muslims (the majority of maintstream Muslims in the World) normally follow one of 4 schools of *Sunni fiqh* (i.e. Jurisprudence), established by four respected *imams* (or leaders of fiqh): Abu Hanifah, Malek, Ash-Shafii and Ahmed ibn Hanbal (died 241 H). These four imams follow one of the above three opinions.

According to the majority of Muslim scholars, the Opening should be read by the *imam* (leader of prayers) or by a person praying by himself in every *rakaa* (literally meaning bowing down) during prayer. The Opening (sometimes followed by another complete sura or some ayas) is read before bowing down. There are 17 compulsory rakaas in a day spread over 5 compulsory prayers at specified times during one day, two rakaas at Al-Fajr, four at Al-Dhuhr, four at Al-Asr, three at Al-Maghreb and four at Al-Isha.

Muslims who consider the Basmalah as part of the Opening read it, while those who do not consider it so may omit reading it. Malek says it should not be read in the compulsory prayers but may be read in the non-compulsory ones. Abu Hanifah and Ahmed bin Hanbal say it should be read before the Opening in every rakaa of any prayer but silently, without it being heard. Ash-Shafii on the other hand says it should be read loudly in the loud rakaas and silently in the silent rakaas [62]. The loud rakaas are the two rakaas of Al-Fajr, the first two rakaas of Al-Maghreb and the first two rakaas of Al-Isha compulsory prayers. The loud rakaas have to be read loudly by the imam but a person praying by himself may choose to read loudly or silently.

The word *bismi* بسم (in the name) appears in the Quran in three ayas (or verses) in the Arabic script form consisting of 3 letters namely: *ba, seen* and *meem*. It appears as باسم, also pronounced *bismi,* in four ayas in the form consisting of 4 letters namely: *ba, alef, seen* and *meem.* In all the first three cases the word is followed by the word Allah. In all the 4 other cases it is followed by the word ربك (your Lord). Although the two forms of the Arabic word are identical in sound, according to some interpreters, the reason for the shorter form before the word Allah is to enable the reader to reach Allah faster. This is one of the proofs that the script of the Quran is *tawqeefi* (i.e. ordained) by Allah.

Muslims believe that the translation of the Quran is impossible because it consists of words of Allah and is both a linguistic and literary miracle. The Quran also contains many scientific facts which were not known to humanity at the time it was revealed, which is one of the other aspects of the miraculousness of the Quran. In fact the Quran states clearly in *Surat Fussilat:*

$$سَنُرِيهِمْ ءَايَٰتِنَا فِى ٱلْءَافَاقِ وَفِىٓ أَنفُسِهِمْ حَتَّىٰ يَتَبَيَّنَ لَهُمْ أَنَّهُ ٱلْحَقُّ أَوَلَمْ يَكْفِ بِرَبِّكَ أَنَّهُۥ عَلَىٰ كُلِّ شَىْءٍ شَهِيدٌ ۝٥٣$$

(فصلت/53)

"We will show them Our signs in the horizons and within themselves until it becomes clear to them that it is the truth. But is it not sufficient concerning your Lord that He is, over all things, a Witness?"

Surat Fusilat, Ayah 53. [63].

All translations are, therefore, merely attempts to translate the meanings of the Quran.

Bismillah is translated in many available translations of the meanings of the Quran as: "In the name of God". However the word God does not convey the full meaning of the one and only God: Allah. God is a word which has the plural gods, whereas Allah is an Arabic word that does not take a plural. God could be translated in Arabic as *ilah,* and gods as *alihah.* Hence it is more accurate to translate Bismillah as "In the name of Allah". Allah is considered the greatest name of God who has ninety nine names according to one *hadith* (or saying) by the Prophet (ﷺ).

عَنْ أَبِي هُرَيْرَةَ، رِوَايَةً قَالَ " لِلَّهِ تِسْعَةٌ وَتِسْعُونَ اسْمًا، مِائَةٌ إِلاَّ وَاحِدًا، لاَ يَحْفَظُهَا أَحَدٌ إِلاَّ دَخَلَ الْجَنَّةَ، وَهْوَ وَتْرٌ يُحِبُّ الْوَتْرَ ".

Narrated Abu Huraira: Allah has ninety-nine Names, i.e., one hundred minus one, and whoever believes in their meanings and acts accordingly, will enter Paradise; and Allah is witr (one) and loves 'the witr' (i.e., odd numbers). Sahih al-Bukhari 6410, In-Book reference: Book 80, Hadith 105 [64]

Moreover, in its essence the name Allah is inherently monotheistic! Some Muslims (or Moslems) writing in English prefer to use the word God rather than Allah to avoid the misunderstanding in the mind of some non-Muslims who imagine that Allah is the God of Muslims and/ or Arabs only. We hope that we have made it clear that Allah means the "One and Only God" of all beings and every thing in existence.

The next word in the Basmalah is *Ar-Rahman*. Going through more than 30 published translations of the meanings of the Quran, this has been translated as: The Merciful, Most Merciful, The All Merciful, The Mercy-giving, The Source of Mercy, Beneficent, The Beneficent, The Most Beneficent, Compassionate, The Compassionate and Most Gracious, The Infinitely Good. An approximation may be the Source of Infinite Mercy. However, none of these words or phrases fully conveys the meaning of the word which in our opinion is untranslatable, and therefore, like the word Allah, should remain as Ar-Rahman. Aya 110 of Surat Al-Isra' in the Quran starts:

$$قُلِ ادْعُوا اللَّهَ أَوِ ادْعُوا الرَّحْمَٰنَ أَيًّا مَّا تَدْعُوا فَلَهُ الْأَسْمَاءُ الْحُسْنَىٰ وَلَا تَجْهَرْ بِصَلَاتِكَ وَلَا تُخَافِتْ بِهَا وَابْتَغِ بَيْنَ ذَٰلِكَ سَبِيلًا ﴿١١٠﴾$$

(الإسراء/110)

"Say, "Call upon Allah or call upon the Ar-Rahman. Whichever (name) you call - to Him belong the Best Names." And do not recite (too) loudly in your prayer or [too] quietly but seek between that an (intermediate) way."

Surat Al Isra (The Assesnsation), Ayah 110 [65].

It is a word in Arabic which is only applied to Allah and is a word which was not generally known to the Arabs before Islam and the revelation of the Quran. Aya 60 of *Surat Al-Furqan* starts:

$$وَإِذَا قِيلَ لَهُمُ اسْجُدُوا لِلرَّحْمَٰنِ قَالُوا وَمَا الرَّحْمَٰنُ أَنَسْجُدُ لِمَا تَأْمُرُنَا وَزَادَهُمْ نُفُورًا ۩ ﴿٦٠﴾$$

(الفرقان/60)

"And when it is said to them, "Prostrate to the Ar-Rahman" they say, "And what is the Ar-Rahman. Should we prostrate to that which you order us?" And it increases them in aversion."

Surat Al Furqan (The Criterian), Ayah 60 [66].

Ar-Rahman has a special place amongst the 99 names of Allah and comes immediately after it. There is also a sura that is called Ar-Rahman and starts with that very word. Al-Rahman appears in the Quran 45 times if we do not include its appearance in the 112

67

Basmalahs mentioned above. Interestingly it appears in *Surat Mariyam* (The Virgin Mary (PBUH)) eleven times (not counting the Basmallah as an aya that is a part of this sura) where the name of God, Allah appears mostly as Ar-Rahman.

Allah, relays in many ayas of *Surat Al-Furqan* a description of those who are the servants of Ar-Rahman:

$$\text{وَعِبَادُ ٱلرَّحْمَٰنِ ٱلَّذِينَ يَمْشُونَ عَلَى ٱلْأَرْضِ هَوْنًا وَإِذَا خَاطَبَهُمُ ٱلْجَٰهِلُونَ قَالُوا۟ سَلَٰمًا ٦٣}$$

(الفرقان/63)

[And the servants of the Ar-Rahman are those who walk upon the earth easily, and when the ignorant address them [harshly], they say [words of] peace]
Surat Al Furqan (The Criterian), Ayah 63 [67].

Another possible translation would be: those worshippers who tread softly on earth and when the ignorant (or unwise) address them, they reply with a peaceful response.

Musailimah the Liar, one of those who claimed prophethood, was the only person to call himself Rahman and hence he is permanently punished by having the word "Liar" always attached to his name whenever he is mentioned by Muslims. Musailimah was killed in the *Ridda Wars* in the days of Abu Bakr As-Siddeeq (MABPWH) the first Caliph (Khalifa) who ruled the Muslims immediately after the Prophet (ﷺ). When the Egyptian poet Mahmoud Abbas Al-Aqqad (1889-1964) wrote in one of his poems a line that says:

والشعر من نفس الرحمن مقتبس   والشاعر الفذ بين الناس رحمن

i.e. Poetry is obtained (like a flame) from the soul of Ar-Rahman, and the great poet is a Rahman amongst people, he was strongly criticized as the word Rahman is exclusive to Allah.

The last word of the *Basmalah* is Ar-Raheem which means The Most Merciful. The various translations available used some of the following words or phrases to translate it: *Merciful, The Merciful, Most Merciful, The Most Merciful, The All Merciful, Ever Merciful, Mercy Giving, The Compassionate, The All compassionate and The Dispenser of Grace.* Unlike the word Rahman, the word or adjective Raheem (merciful) may be applied to people.

Both the words Ar-Rahman and Ar-Raheem come from the same root. Rahmah means mercy. One hadith states:

عن عبدالرحمن بن عوف رضي الله عنه أن النبي صلى الله عليه وسلم

قال: قَالَ اللَّهُ عَزَّ وَجَلَّ أَنَا الرَّحْمَنُ خَلَقْتُ الرَّحِمَ وَشَقَقْتُ لَهَا مِنْ اسْمِي

فَمَنْ يَصِلُهَا أَصِلُهُ وَمَنْ يَقْطَعُهَا أَقْطَعُهُ فَأَبُتَّهُ... (رواه أحمد)

Abdur-Rahman bin Auf (MABPWH) said that the Prophet (ﷺ) said: Allah, Mighty and Majestic is He, said: *"I am Ar-Rahman and I created the rahem (i.e. womb) and derived a name for it from my name. So he who connects with it We will connect with him, and he who severs from it We will sever from him and alienate him"* (Narrated by Ahmed) [68].

The reference here is to relatives and the fundamental requirement from Muslims to be good to them and to maintain contact with them.

In his interpretation of the Quran, Ibn Jareer At-Tabari (died 310 H) says that Allah is Ar-Rahman for all creatures (by providing for them in this world) but He is Ar-Raheem only for the believers in Allah (by giving them guidance). The structure of the word Rahman denotes abundance of rahmah i.e. mercy or the very limit of mercy. Rahman is a name specific to Allah but its bounty encompasses believers and non-believers in this world, whereas Raheem is a name or adjective not specific to Allah as it can describe a person, but Allah is Raheem for the believers only. The Quran says:

$$\text{هُوَ ٱلَّذِى يُصَلِّى عَلَيْكُمْ وَمَلَـٰٓئِكَتُهُۥ لِيُخْرِجَكُم مِّنَ ٱلظُّلُمَـٰتِ إِلَى ٱلنُّورِ ۚ وَكَانَ بِٱلْمُؤْمِنِينَ رَحِيمًا ﴿٤٣﴾}$$

(الأحزاب/ 43)

"He it is Who sends Salat (His blessings) on you, and His angels too (ask Allah to bless and forgive you), that He may bring you out from darkness (of disbelief and polytheism) into light (of belief and Islamic Monotheism) And He is Ever Most Merciful to the believers".

Surat Al-Ahzab (The Confoderates), Ayah 43. [69].

Muslims are supposed to say the Basmalah before reading the Quran. In one testimony [74] when the Quran was first revealed to the Prophet (ﷺ) by A *Jibreel* (Archangel Gabriel) (PBUH), the first aya was:

$$\text{ٱقْرَأْ بِٱسْمِ رَبِّكَ ٱلَّذِى خَلَقَ ﴿١﴾}$$

(العلق/1)

"Recite in the name of your Lord who created".

Surat Al-Alaq, Ayah 1. [70].

Muslims are also supposed to say the Basmalah before they do their ablution (for prayer, or for reading the Quran, etc.), before entering their house, before eating or drinking, before slaughtering an animal for food and even before sex with their spouses. Muslims usually start their public speeches, their letters and many of their actions with the Basmalah, i.e. in the name of Allah. This reminds a Muslim of Allah and that he relies on Him, and that he lives to worship and obey him, and exists in His pleasure. Starting an act in the name of Allah means that you are by default planning to do something that is not supposed to displease Him. According to a hadith mentioned in Tafseer Ibn Katheer كل أمر لا يبدأ فيه ببسم الله الرحمن الرحيم فهو أجذم .i.e "Any matter not started by the Basmalah is cut off or mutilated". Islam is truly a way of life.

In conclusion we suggest that the aya discussed in this chapter is to be translated as follows: **"In the Name of Allah, the *Rahman* (the source of endless and absolute Mercy), the Most Merciful".**

Chapter 5

الْحَمْدَلَه: الْحَمْدُ لِلَّهِ رَبِّ الْعَالَمِين

Al Hamdalah: Al Hamdu Lillah Rabil Alameen

The verse الْحَمْد للَّهِ رَبِّ الْعَالَمِين is known for short as Al-Hamdalah i.e. Al-Hamd li-Allah Rab Al-Alameen, pronounced Al-Hamdu lillah Rabil Alameen.

As discussed in our chapter on Al-Fatihah, one of the many names of Al-Fatihah is actually *Al-Hamd*. This is based on the first word of the first verse following the *Basmallah* verse. In fact, that verse, which is the title of this chapter, (starting with the word a*l-hamd)* is according to some scholars the actual first verse of the first sura of the Nobel Quran, arguing that the Basmalah is only for blessing. It is interesting to note that the Prophet (ﷺ) started all his written messages with the Basmalah but started all his spoken sermons with the Hamdalah.

The verse is made up in Arabic of only 4 words, but while reviewing more than 30 translations of the meanings of the Quran, we have found the translations of the meanings of this verse ranging from 8 to 32 English words. Some translators felt the need to elaborate more to cover and encompass as much of the meaning as possible. However, most of the translators went for the shorter concise approximate translation of the meaning. The variations in the available translations of this verse are much greater than the translations of *Al-Basmallah* verse.

The first word is *al-hamd* and its translations can be grouped from the above translations as: praise, all praise, all types of perfect praise, all the praise and thanks, all praise and gratitude (whoever gives them to whomever for whatever reason and in whatever way from the first day of creation until eternity). This last phrase is obviously an attempt by the translator, Ali Unal [71] to provide a more comprehensive interpretation. Ibn Ajibah [72] explains that al-hamd is praise with the intention to applaud greatness (*Ta'dheem*) تعظيم and salutations (*Tabheel*) تبهيل and this directed by the servant of Allah by choice in admiration to the great attributes both known and incomprehensible to the limited human mind.

The word al-hamdالحمد (i.e. praise) is different from the word *al-shukr* الشكر (pronounced ash-shukr) (i.e. thanks or gratitude) in that al-shukr is said in return for a deed whereas al-hamd is for the acts of giving by choice, and also for the attributes of the one praised, in this case Allah. In Arabic if the praise is for giving not by choice but by nature, the word *al-madh*المدح is used, which consists of the same letters as those of al-hamd but in a different arrangement as happens in many Arabic words with the meanings of the words remaining related. Thus praising the beauty of a woman or of the scenery would be madh and not hamd. In Arabic, al-hamd is most often used in praising Allah, and thus the word praise as offered in translation cannot convey this almost exclusivity. Thus some commentators/translators have chosen to translate it as *"Praise is only to Allah"*.

The second word in the verse is *li-Allah* لله (pronounced *lillah*). *Li* in Arabic is a single letter preposition meaning for or to, which is attached to the following noun, in this case Allah. Allah is considered the most commonly used name of God. The concept of Allah conveys the centrality of the Divine Who is the All Provider and within Whose realm and authority every thing exists, to the exclusion of any other authority or power.

However, what should be appreciated is that Muslims use *al-Hamdu-lillah* (i.e. al-hamd li-Allah) meaning Praise to Allah at all times and circumstances. Thus a Muslim would use it at times of happiness, prosperity, and success, but also at times of sadness, bad luck and at difficult and tough times such as illness or the death of a dear person. In fact, the *al-hamd* being a compulsory verse in all prayers confirms the very basic expectation to thank and praise God for everything, anything, anywhere, everywhere and at any and all times borne from that strong covenant between the servant and Master, i.e. the believer and Allah (SWT). This fulfils as such the basic tenant of Islam when the Muslim bears witness that there is no God but Allah (SWT) and thus surrenders and accepts fully what the Lord has planned and given to him – and thanks and praises Him under all these conditions and circumstances.

In his Nobel Prize speech Bertrand Russel says: *"It is scarcely possible to exaggerate the influence of vanity throughout the range of human life, from the child of three to the potentate at whose frown the world trembles. Mankind have even committed the impiety of attributing similar desires to the Deity, whom they imagine avid for continual praise".* [73]. But it is the Quran itself that starts Al-Fatihah, after the Basmalah, with "Praise to Allah". In Surat Al-Dhariat, verse 56 the Quran states:

$$وَمَا خَلَقْتُ الْجِنَّ وَالْإِنسَ إِلَّا لِيَعْبُدُونِ ۝$$

(الذاريات/56)

"And I did not create the jinn and mankind except to worship Me"
Al Dhariyat, Ayah 56. [74]

Muslims believe that the Quran comes to comfort and befriend the believer even after death in his grave and in heaven. In Surat Saba verse no 1 the Quran says:

$$الْحَمْدُ لِلَّهِ الَّذِي لَهُ مَا فِي السَّمَاوَاتِ وَمَا فِي الْأَرْضِ وَلَهُ الْحَمْدُ فِي الْآخِرَةِ وَهُوَ الْحَكِيمُ الْخَبِيرُ ۝$$

(سبأ/1)

"(All) praise is (due) to Allah, to whom belongs whatever is in the heavens and whatever is in the earth, and to Him belongs (all) praise in the Hereafter. And He is the Wise, the Acquainted."

Surat Saba, Ayah 1, [75].

The phrase "al-hamd li-Allah" appears in 20 verses other than Al-Fatihah which almost every practicing Muslim memorizes regardless of knowing or remembering by heart any other parts and verses of the Quran. This is because he/she needs it in all his/her compulsory and voluntary prayers. In reality there are huge numbers of Muslims who have been blessed with memorizing the whole Noble Quran. *Juma* i.e. Friday prayer sermons are usually started with the phrase "al-hamd li-Allah".

In Al-Fatihah Al-Hamdalah comes immediately after the Basmalah and says:

ٱلْحَمْدُ لِلَّهِ رَبِّ ٱلْعَٰلَمِينَ ۝

(الفاتحة/2)

"Praise be to Allah, the Cherisher and Sustainer of the worlds"
Surat Al-Fatihah, Ayah 2. [76]

There are 4 suras in the Quran that start with "Al hamad li-Allah" (other than its appearance in Al-Fatihah) namely: Al-Anam, Al-Kahf, Saba, and Fatir. In Surat Al-Anam the first verse is:

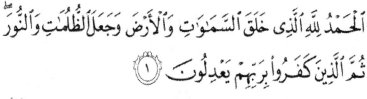

(الأنعام/1)

"(All) praise is (due) to Allah, who created the heavens and the earth and made the darkness and the light. Yet those who disbelieve equate [others] with their Lord."

Surat Al An'am, Ayah 1 [77]

The first verse of Surat Al-Kahf states:

$$\text{ٱلْحَمْدُ لِلَّهِ ٱلَّذِىٓ أَنزَلَ عَلَىٰ عَبْدِهِ ٱلْكِتَٰبَ وَلَمْ يَجْعَل لَّهُۥ عِوَجَا ۜ}$$

(الكهف/1)

"(All) praise is (due) to Allah, who has sent down upon His Servant the Book and has not made therein any deviance crookedness?

Al Kahf (The Cave), 1. [78]

The first verse of Surat Saba says:

$$\text{ٱلْحَمْدُ لِلَّهِ ٱلَّذِى لَهُۥ مَا فِى ٱلسَّمَٰوَٰتِ وَمَا فِى ٱلْأَرْضِ وَلَهُ ٱلْحَمْدُ فِى ٱلْءَاخِرَةِ ۚ وَهُوَ ٱلْحَكِيمُ ٱلْخَبِيرُ}$$

(سبأ/1)

"(All) praise is (due) to Allah, to whom belongs whatever is in the heavens and whatever is in the earth, and to Him belongs (all) praise in the Hereafter. And He is the Wise, the Acquainted."

Surat Saba, Ayah 1, [79].

And the first verse of Surat Fatir states:

$$\text{ٱلْحَمْدُ لِلَّهِ فَاطِرِ ٱلسَّمَٰوَٰتِ وَٱلْأَرْضِ جَاعِلِ ٱلْمَلَٰٓئِكَةِ رُسُلًا أُو۟لِىٓ أَجْنِحَةٍ مَّثْنَىٰ وَثُلَٰثَ وَرُبَٰعَ ۚ يَزِيدُ فِى ٱلْخَلْقِ مَا يَشَآءُ ۚ إِنَّ ٱللَّهَ عَلَىٰ كُلِّ شَىْءٍ قَدِيرٌ}$$

(فاطر/1)

"(All) praise is (due) to Allah, Creator of the heavens and the earth, [who] made the angels messengers having wings, two or three or four. He increases in creation what He wills. Indeed, Allah is over all things competent"

Surat Fatir, Ayah 1. [80]

The expression "Al hamad li-Allah" also appears in the last verse of three suras namely Al-Isra, An-Naml and Az-Zumar.

The third word in the verse is *Rab*. In Arabic this word can cover several meanings. According to Mawdudi the word rather bridges a broad-based concept that covers the following range of meanings [81]:

- He Who nourishes and dispenses needs, brings up morally and physically.
- He Who takes care, supervises, and is responsible for improving.
- He Who has the axial position upon whom divergence converges.
- He Who is the noblest and the source of power and authority: Whose writ prevails and Who is the wielder of dispensation.
- He Who is the owner and the master.

In the Quran the use of the word *Rab* (رب) involves all the above meanings in different verses. Sometimes it involves one or two of the above meanings and in other cases embrace several of these meanings. In the verse under discussion the main meaning of the word is Lord, Owner and Master. What is referred to here is the concept of *"Rubbubiyah"* (ربوبية) which is the Lordship/Ownership of Allah of All the worlds, but also all the other concepts above.

The word Rab in Arabic is never used in its singular form except to mean Allah (SWT). As such the word Lord or Master is an English translation, and as such if the verse said Alhamd li-Allah Al-Rab, then it would have automatically meant God. However, if the word rab is used as lord or master to mean a person, then we say rab al-manzel to mean master of the house, or rab al-bustan as the Master of the Garden, and so on.

In verses 3 and 4 of Surat Quraish the Quran states:

$$فَلْيَعْبُدُوا رَبَّ هَذَا الْبَيْتِ ۝٣$$

$$الَّذِي أَطْعَمَهُم مِّن جُوعٍ وَءَامَنَهُم مِّنْ خَوْفٍ ۝٤$$

(قريش/ 3-4)

"Let them worship the Lord of this House".
"Who has fed them, [saving them] from hunger and made them safe, (saving them) from fear"
Surat Quraysh, Ayah 3-4. [82]

The Rab being the ultimate and absolute Master, Lord, Sustainer, He and thus He alone is worthy of having the title. He has created man and all other creatures and everything in existence including the non-living, and it is with that He is worshiped. Rab can also mean that Allah (SWT) is the Cherisher; Sustainer, Sovereign, Judge and True Owner of all existence.

The fourth word in the verse is *Al-Alameen* العالمين. This is a plural of the word a*alam* عالم i.e. world. The word in Arabic come from the root word عَلِمَ *alima* (to know). The word عِلْم *elm* means knowledge. The Lord Allah (SWT) Who by default possesses knowledge of all that exists in its absolute entirety. *Alameen* is a term used only in the Quran, and is used to encompass all the different worlds in their diversities, their differing sizes and complexities, including the world of angels, the world of humans, the world of jinn, the world of animals, the world of plants, etc. Many scholars have spoken of the various different infinitely enormous number of worlds those from the sub-atomic and nuclear levels to the "at-large"" cosmic levels to encompass the heavens and beyond, and in fact, **everything other than Allah Himself**. The word

78

alam can also be used here to have connotations that relate to the Arabic word علامة *alamah* which means mark or sign, and as such for the worlds or parts of the universe that mankind has been able to explore.

Like Allah and Al Rahman, *Rab al-alameen* is a term unique to the one and only God. It appears in the Quran 34 times out of which 9 times in Surat Al-Shu'ara الشعراء. In Verses 23 to 28 of that sura an epic dialogue between Pharaoh and Moses (PBUH) takes place in which Pharaoh questions Moses (BPUH) about *Rab al-alameen*:

قَالَ فِرْعَوْنُ وَمَا رَبُّ ٱلْعَٰلَمِينَ ﴿٢٣﴾

قَالَ رَبُّ ٱلسَّمَٰوَٰتِ وَٱلْأَرْضِ وَمَا بَيْنَهُمَا ۖ إِن كُنتُم مُّوقِنِينَ ﴿٢٤﴾

قَالَ لِمَنْ حَوْلَهُ أَلَا تَسْتَمِعُونَ ﴿٢٥﴾

قَالَ رَبُّكُمْ وَرَبُّ ءَابَآئِكُمُ ٱلْأَوَّلِينَ ﴿٢٦﴾

قَالَ إِنَّ رَسُولَكُمُ ٱلَّذِىٓ أُرْسِلَ إِلَيْكُمْ لَمَجْنُونٌ ﴿٢٧﴾

قَالَ رَبُّ ٱلْمَشْرِقِ وَٱلْمَغْرِبِ وَمَا بَيْنَهُمَآ ۖ إِن كُنتُمْ تَعْقِلُونَ ﴿٢٨﴾

(الشعراء/23-28)

"Said Pharaoh, "And what is the Lord of the worlds?""
"(Moses) said, "The Lord of the heavens and earth and that between them, if you should be convinced.""
"(Pharaoh) said to those around him, "Do you not hear?""
"(Moses) said, "Your Lord and the Lord of your first forefathers.""
"(Pharaoh) said, "Indeed, your 'messenger' who has been sent to you is mad.""

"(Moses) said, "Lord of the east and the west and that between them, if you were to reason.""

Surat Al Shu'ara, Ayat 23-28 [83]

These verses describe the "Rububiyah" i.e. Lordship concept through this dialogue between a prophet and one of the most arrogant and obtuse disbelievers on earth!

Thus the meaning of the aya:

الْحَمْدُ لِلَّهِ رَبِّ الْعَالَمِينَ ۝

is Praise to Allah and recognizing that He is the Lord and Master of everything in the universe and in the hereafter, i.e. everything other than Allah Himself. We as mankind must admit our subservience to the Lord (SWT), and it is only most appropriate to start the prayers by thanking Him for our very existence which has come about only by His wish. Moreover our continued existence is only possible by His sustaining us. Thus we start our prayer in His name by the Basmallah as explained in the previous chapter, and then by all absolute and complete praise to Him and to Him alone. This is again a central theme in Islam being a solid monotheistic faith. Although we cannot directly see Allah physically creating or sustaining, neither can we see all the worlds, yet as Muslims we bear witness to the existence of Allah and الغيب i.e. all the Unseen (such as the Angels, Heaven and Hell etc.) and thus we call Him as Rab Al-Alameen. **Al-alameen is thus everything in existence other than Allah (SWT).**

Given the discussion above perhaps an approximate translation of the meanings of this could be: ***"All absolute and perfect praise is only ultimately and truly attributed to Allah, the Master and Sustainer of all absolute existence (all worlds – i.e. everything in existence other than Allah (SWT)"***.

Chapter 6

الرَّحْمَنِ الرَّحِيم

Ar-Rahman Ar-Raheem

We have already come across the phrase Ar-Rahman Ar-Raheem as part of the Basmalah which is accepted by the majority of muslim scholars to be the first aya of Al-Fatihah. But now it comes as the third aya of Al-Fatihah. The fact that it comes again so soon after the Basmalah, was one of the main reasons that led scholars such as At-Tabari [84], who is one of the first major interpreters of the Quran, to believe that the Basmalah is not part of Al-Fatihah. He argued that repetition with no ayas of a different meaning in between does not exist in the Quran. Of course there is one aya, which is *al-hamdalah* in between, but At-Tabari argues, in a rather complicated linguistic argument why he does not consider that aya to be a real separating aya. He says that a number of interpreters consider that *Ar-Rahman Ar-Raheem* has been located in this position but in meaning belongs to an earlier word position in the middle of the previous aya, as if the two ayas read as: "Al-Hamd li-Allah *Ar-Rahman Ar-Raheem* Rab Al-Alameen". He argued that this is common in Arabic and gave an example from the Quran itself, namely from the first two ayas of Surat Al-Kahf i.e.

الْحَمْدُ لِلّهِ الَّذِى أَنزَلَ عَلَى عَبْدِهِ الْكِتَبَ وَلَمْ يَجْعَل لَّهُۥ عِوَجَاۜ ۝

قَيِّمًا لِّيُنذِرَ بَأْسًا شَدِيدًا مِّن لَّدُنْهُ وَيُبَشِّرَ ٱلْمُؤْمِنِينَ ٱلَّذِينَ
يَعْمَلُونَ ٱلصَّٰلِحَٰتِ أَنَّ لَهُمْ أَجْرًا حَسَنًا ۝

"(All) praise is (due) to Allah, who has sent down upon His Servant the Book and has not made therein any deviance (crookedness)."
"(He has made it) straight, to warn of severe punishment from Him and to give good tidings to the believers who do righteous deeds that they will have a good reward."

Suart Al Kahf, Ayat 1-2 [85]

At-Tabari also stated that in "Al-Hamd li-Allah *Ar-Rahman Ar-Raheem Rab Al-Alameen*", Rab Al-Alameen would now would logically be followed by Malik or Malek Yawm Ad-Din, (whichever of the two acceptable readings of the word), a phrase which describes Rab Al-Alameen. But this opinion of Al-Tabari related to Al-Basmalah does not represent the mainstream opinion. We already discussed the three different opinions concerning the Basmalah.

If we exclude the Basmalah at the beginning of the sura we find that the phrase *Ar-Rahman Ar-Raheem* appears in the Noble Quran other than in Al-Fatihah in 4 other suras. These ayas and their translation are given below:

(1) In Surat Al-Baqarah, Ayah163:

وَإِلَٰهُكُمْ إِلَٰهٌ وَٰحِدٌ لَّآ إِلَٰهَ إِلَّا هُوَ ٱلرَّحْمَٰنُ ٱلرَّحِيمُ ۝

(البقرة/163)

"And your god is one God. There is no deity (worthy of worship) except Him, the Rahman (the Entirely Merciful), the Especially Merciful."

Surat Al Baqarah (The Cow), Ayah 163 [86]

(2) In Surat An-Naml, Ayah 30:

$$إِنَّهُۥ مِن سُلَيۡمَـٰنَ وَإِنَّهُۥ بِسۡمِ ٱللَّهِ ٱلرَّحۡمَـٰنِ ٱلرَّحِيمِ ۝٣٠$$

(النمل/30)

"Indeed, it is from Solomon, and indeed, it reads: 'In the name of Allah, the Rahman (the Entirely Merciful), the Especially Merciful"
Surat Al Naml (The Ants), Ayah 30 [87].

(3) In Surat Fusilat, Ayah 2:

$$تَنزِيلٌ مِّنَ ٱلرَّحۡمَـٰنِ ٱلرَّحِيمِ ۝٢$$

(فصلت/2)

"(This is) a revelation from the Rahman (the Entirely Merciful), the Especially Merciful"
Surat Fusilat, Ayah 2. [88]

(4) In suat Al-Hashr, Ayah 22:

$$هُوَ ٱللَّهُ ٱلَّذِى لَآ إِلَـٰهَ إِلَّا هُوَ عَـٰلِمُ ٱلۡغَيۡبِ وَٱلشَّهَـٰدَةِ هُوَ ٱلرَّحۡمَـٰنُ ٱلرَّحِيمُ ۝٢٢$$

(الحشر/22)

"He is Allah, other than whom there is no deity, Knower of the unseen and the witnessed. He is the Rahman (the Entirely Merciful), the Especially Merciful."
Surat Al Hashr, Ayah 22. [89].

We have already argued in the Basmalah chapter that *Ar-Rahman* is not translatable and should, therefore, remain in its Arabic form. It is a word in Arabic which is applied only to Allah and is a word which was generally not known to the Arabs before Islam and the revelation of the Quran. The major classical Arabic dictionary Lisan Al-Arab states that, according to Abu Al-Hasan, it is a word that was in the books of earlier prophets, but he does not elaborate or give any evidence of this. The word means one with compassion and mercy beyond any compassion and mercy. Ar-Rahman has a special place amongst the commonly known 99 names of Allah and comes immediately after the name Allah itself. This is cofirmed by the aya 110 of Surat Al-Isra' in the Quran where Allah associated the name Ar-Rahman with his most sacred name i.e. "Allah". The aya says:

$$قُلِ ٱدْعُواْ ٱللَّهَ أَوِ ٱدْعُواْ ٱلرَّحْمَٰنَ ۖ أَيًّا مَّا تَدْعُواْ فَلَهُ ٱلْأَسْمَآءُ ٱلْحُسْنَىٰ ۚ وَلَا تَجْهَرْ بِصَلَاتِكَ وَلَا تُخَافِتْ بِهَا وَٱبْتَغِ بَيْنَ ذَٰلِكَ سَبِيلًا ﴿١١٠﴾$$

(الإسراء/110)

"Say, "Call upon Allah or call upon the Rahman (the Entirely Merciful). Whichever (name) you call - to Him belong the best names." And do not recite (too) loudly in your prayer or (too) quietly but seek between that an [intermediate] way"

Surat Al-Isra (The Assesation), 110 [90].

A hadith related by Al-Bukhari states:

$$لِلَّهِ تِسْعَةٌ وَتِسْعُونَ اسْمًا مِائَةٌ إِلَّا وَاحِدًا لَا يَحْفَظُهَا أَحَدٌ إِلَّا دَخَلَ الْجَنَّةَ$$

$$وَهُوَ وَتْرٌ يُحِبُّ الْوَتْرَ (رواه البخاري)$$

"Allah has ninety-nine names, i.e. one-hundred minus one, and whoever knows them will go to Paradise."

Chapter 6: Ar-Rahman Ar-Raheem

The 99 names are in a hadith narrated by Tirmidhi as related by Abu Hurairah [91] (in what is considered to be a weak hadith). The hadith states:

قال رسول الله صلى الله عليه وسلم إن لله تعالى تسعة وتسعين اسما مائة غير واحد من أحصاها دخل الجنة هو الله الذي لا إله إلا هو الرحمن الرحيم الملك القدوس السلام المؤمن المهيمن العزيز الجبار المتكبر الخالق البارئ المصور الغفار القهار الوهاب الرزاق الفتاح العليم القابض الباسط الخافض الرافع المعز المذل السميع البصير الحكم العدل اللطيف الخبير الحليم العظيم الغفور الشكور العلي الكبير الحفيظ المقيت الحسيب الجليل الكريم الرقيب المجيب الواسع الحكيم الودود المجيد الباعث الشهيد الحق الوكيل القوي المتين الولي الحميد المحصي المبدئ المعيد المحي المميت الحي القيوم الواجد الماجد الواحد الصمد القادر المقتدر المقدم المؤخر الأول الآخر الظاهر الباطن الوالي المتعالي البر التواب المنتقم العفو الرءوف مالك الملك ذو الجلال والإكرام المقسط الجامع الغني المغني المانع الضار النافع النور الهادي البديع الباقي الوارث الرشيد الصبور.

A translation of this hadith reads: Allaah's Messenger (ﷺ) said: *"Allaah The Most High has ninety-nine names. He who retains them in his memory will enter Paradise. He is Allaah, other than whom there is none worthy of worship, the Compassionate, the Merciful, the King, the Holy, the Source of Peace, the Preserver of Security, the Protector, the Mighty, the Overpowering, the Great in Majesty, the Creator, the Maker, the Fashioner, the Forgiver, the Dominant, the Bestower, the Provider, the Decider, the Knower, the Withholder, the Plentiful Giver, the Abaser, the Exalted, the Honourer, the Humiliator, the Hearer, the Seer, the Judge, the Just, the Gracious, the Informed, the Clement, the Incomparably Great, the Forgiving, the Rewarder, the Most High, the Most Great, the Preserver, the Sustainer, the Reckoner, the Majestic, the Generous, the Watcher, the Answerer, the Liberal, the Wise, the Loving, the Glorious, the Raiser, the Witness, the Real, the Trustee, the Strong, the Firm, the Patron, the Praiseworthy, the All-Knowing, the Originator, the Restorer to Life, the Giver of Life, the Giver of Death, the*

Living, the Eternal, the Self-sufficient, the Grand, the One, the Single, He to Whom men repair, the Powerful, the Prevailing, the Advancer, the Delayer, the First, the Last, the Outward, the Inward, the Governor, the Sublime, the Amply Beneficent, the Acceptor of Repentance, the Avenger, the Pardoner, the Kindly, the Ruler of the Kingdom, the Lord of Majesty and Splendor, the Equitable, the Gatherer, the Independent, the Enricher, the Depriver, the Harmer, the Benefactor, the Light, the Guide, the First Cause, the Enduring, the Inheritor, the Director, the Patient."

Ibn Majah also related a similar hadith with a few differences in the names. However, both the hadiths are considered weak and that is probably why al-Bukhari and Muslim did not include them in their Sahihs. There is, however, a consensus among scholars that Allah's names are not confined to ninety nine but there are many more. But the only names and attributes to be ascribed to Allah are those mentioned in the Quran or in the authentic Sunnah as these are directly communicated to us and are not the products of opinion and interpretation [92].

The other word in the aya is *Ar-Raheem* which means The Merciful. As explained earlier, the word Raheem, unlike the word Rahman, may be applied to people. Raheem is an exaggerated form of the word Rahem راحم, i.e. merciful, but Ar-Rahman is the ultimate form of exaggeration of the word. Normally in describing someone, one would proceed from the less strong attribute to the stronger one, and once one starts with the stronger attribute there would be no need to use the lesser one. Here the purpose of the use of Ar-Raheem after the more exaggerated form Ar-Rahman is explained by some interpreters as the addition of the finer details of mercy to the main aspects of mercy already covered by the word Ar-Rahman. Lisan Al-Arab also states that Al-Azhari related that Abu Al-Abbas said that Ar-Rahman is a Hebrew word while Ar-Raheem is Arabic, and Allah used the two words together for greater effect.

Chapter 6: Ar-Rahman Ar-Raheem

In the chapter about Al-Basmalah we mentioned that the mercy and bounty of Al-Rahman encompasses believers and non-believers, whereas the mercy and bounty of Ar-Raheem is specifically only for the believers. It is also said that Allah is Ar-Rahman of/in this world and also the hereafter, whereas He is Ar-Raheem of/in this world: i.e. رحمن الدنيا والآخرة ورحيم الدنيا.

Given the above discussion, an approximate translation of the meaning of "Ar-Rahman Ar-Raheem" could be: ***"The Rahman (the source of endless and absolute Mercy), the Most Merciful."***

Chapter 7

مَالِكِ يَوْمِ الدِّينِ

Maliki Yawm Ad-Deen

This chapter addresses the fourth aya of Al-Fatihah namely مالك يوم الدين "Malik Yawm Ad-Deen", pronounced "Maliki Yawmi-d-Deen". The aya consists of only three words but is of tremendous significance, because it speaks about the day of requital in the Hereafter. Believing in that day is one of the six pillars of *iman* إيمان i.e. faith as we read in a part of a *hadith* in Musnad Ahmed:

.....الإسلام أن تشهد أن لا إله إلا الله وأن محمدا رسول الله وتقيم الصلاة وتؤتي الزكاة وتصوم رمضان وتحج البيت إن استطعت إليه سبيلا قال صدقت قال فعجبنا له يسأله ويصدقه قال ثم قال أخبرني عن الإيمان قال الإيمان أن تؤمن بالله وملائكته وكتبه ورسله واليوم الآخر والقدر كله خيره وشره.... (مسند أحمد)

"..Islam is to bear witness that there is no god by Allah and that Mohammed is his messenger; to pray; to give zakat (alms); fast the holy month of Ramadan and to undertake Haj Pilligramage if you are able to do so, and on the Pillers of Belief (Iman) i.e.: (1) Belief in Allah, (2) His angels, (3) His books, (4) His messengers, (5) the Hereafter, (6) and all Fate and Destiny, good and bad.[93]

In fact the aya has two authentic acceptable forms:

(1) مالك يوم الدين "*Maalik yawm ad-deen*" i.e. the Owner of the day of requital, and

(2) ملك يوم الدين "*Malik yawm ad-deen*" i.e. the Sovereign of the day of requital.

We will herebelow discuss these 3 words and their various meanings in detail.

The first of the three words of the aya is مالك *maalik* or ملك *malik*. Both forms are acceptable and authentic readings. Asem, Al Kisaey and Yaqoob read it as *Maalik* (with the extra *Alif*, which is the first letter of the Arabic alphabet), whilst Nafee, Ibn Katheer, Hamzah, Abu Amr and Ibn Amer read it as *Malik*. Both words are derived from the Arabic past tense verb *Malaka* i.e. owned or possessed. Arabic is a language in which large families of words are derived from a root word. For instance from the verb كتب *kataba* i.e. wrote we derive words such as كتابة *kitabaton* writing, كتاب *Kitab* book, مكتب *maktab* bureau or desk, مكتبة *maktabah* library or bookshop, كاتب *kateb* writer or clerck, إكتتاب *iktitab* subscription, آلة كاتبة *katibah* typewriter, مكتوب *maktoob* letter, مكاتبة *mukatabah* correspondence, and many other words.

Maalik means owner, possessor, lord, or master, whereas *Malik* means king or sovereign. We have reviewed 33 different published English translations of *Al-Fatihah* and found that the translations of the words *Maalik* or *Malik* have been translated into the following: (a) Master – 19 translations; (b) King – 5 translations; (c) Ruler – 3 translations; (d) Owner – 2 translations; (e) The Only Owner & Only Ruling Judge – 1 translation; (f) Possessor – 1 translation; (g) Lord – 1 translation; (h) Sovereign – 1 translation.

In fact, the Glorious Quran refers to Allah (SWT) in one aya as *Maalik* and in another aya as *Malik*. This is another reason that supports the acceptability of both readings. These two ayas are:

قُلِ ٱللَّهُمَّ مَٰلِكَ ٱلْمُلْكِ تُؤْتِى ٱلْمُلْكَ مَن تَشَآءُ وَتَنزِعُ ٱلْمُلْكَ مِمَّن

تَشَآءُ وَتُعِزُّ مَن تَشَآءُ وَتُذِلُّ مَن تَشَآءُ بِيَدِكَ ٱلْخَيْرُ إِنَّكَ عَلَىٰ كُلِّ شَىْءٍ

قَدِيرٌ ٢٦

(آل عمران/26)

"Say, "O Allah, Owner of Sovereignty, You give sovereignty to
whom You will and You take sovereignty away from whom You will.
You honor whom You will and You humble whom You will. In Your
hand is [all] good. Indeed, You have full power over everything."
Surat Aal-Imran, Ayah 26 [94]

In this aya Master or Sovereign of all dominion is a translation of Maalik
al-Mulk. However, the other aya says:

مَٰلِكِ ٱلنَّاسِ ٢

(الناس 2)

"The Sovereign of mankind."

Surat Al-Nas, Ayah 2 [95]

Here *Malik* is used.

The different scholars and interpreters of the Quran have differed in
their preference of choice between the two words *maalik* and *malik*.
Az-Zamakshari (467-538 H) in his classical Quran interpretation (Al-
Kashaf) said that "*Malik*" is more correct as it is the reading of the
people of Al Harameen in Al Hijaz i.e. the two most important centres
of Islam: Makkah and Al Madinah.

In his classical Quran interpretation (Fath Al-Qadeer) Al Shawkani (who
died in 1255 H) said that some interpreters preferred *Malik* as it is more

encompassing than *Maalik* because all kings are owners and yet not all owners are kings, and here Allah owns all and has control overall; but others preferred *Maalik*, as the owner has full control of all what he personally owns. He mentions that Abu Hatem said that *Maalik* is more glorifying in describing Allah, whereas *Malik* is more glorifying in describing humans. [96].

Abu Hamed Al Ghazali (1058-1111) speaks about the beautiful names of Allah. They quote Al Gazhali saying: *"Al Malik or the King is the one who in His essence and attributes has no need of any existing thing, while every existing thing needs Him. There is nothing among things which can dispense with Him concerning anything – whether in the essence or its attributes, its existence or survival; but rather each thing's existence is for Him or for something that is from Him. Everything, other than Him, is subject to Him in its existence and its attributes, while He is independent of everything – and this is what it is to be king absolutely."* [97]

Ibn Jareer At-Tabari in his detailed classical interpretation Jami Al-Bayan fi Tafseer Al-Quran states that *Malik* originates from the word "*Mulk*" which can mean what is within the kingdom, whereas *Maalik* originates from the word "Milk" which is what is owned. [98]

Al Qurtubi (died 671 H) states that both *Malik* and *Maalik* are good and traditionally authentic readings. He also argues that the additional letter in *Maalik* adds to the benefit of the reader/worshiper an extra "*hasanah*" i.e. a good deed as per the *hadith* of the Prophet (ﷺ) related by Al-Tirmidhi:

من قرأ حرفا من كتاب الله فله به حسنة والحسنة بعشر أمثالها لا أقول

الم حرف ولكن ألف حرف ولام حرف وميم حرف (رواه الترمذي)

i.e. he who reads/recites a letter of the Book of Allah (i.e. the Quran) gains one hasanah (a good deed), and the hasanah is multiplied to ten hasanas of its type; I do not say Alef-Lam-Meem a letter, but Alef a letter, Lam a letter and Meem a letter.[99].

In his Al Manar Interpretation of the Quran Sheikh Muhammad Abduh (1849-1905) argued that although Maalik has an extra letter, and that undoubtedly adds more blessings *"hasanat"* in reading, *Malik* has more of an impact on الخشوع *Al Kushoo* which means Reverence/Veneration in prayer when we talk of Kingship. Sheikh Abduh in his book Duroos Mina Al Quran i.e. Lessons from the Quran, again reiterates that *Malik* (King) is more أبلغ *ablagh* i.e. more eloquent, or better because it refers to Sultanship, Strength and Management (*Tadbeer*), whereas *Maalik* may also be considered *ablagh* because it means He is the Master and Owner and has general and overall control. Thus he explains the advantages of each of the two alternatives.[100].

The second word in the aya is يوم *yawm* which means day. This translation of *yawm* is uncontested. Of course the day of requital referred to is not like any other day, and is not necessarily of a duration period of 24 hours like the normal days on our planet. In fact, various ayas in the Quran speak of days of different lengths. Two ayas say that one day with Allah is equal to a thousand earthly years. The first aya is:

$$\text{وَيَسْتَعْجِلُونَكَ بِالْعَذَابِ وَلَن يُخْلِفَ اللَّهُ وَعْدَهُ ۚ وَإِنَّ يَوْمًا عِندَ رَبِّكَ كَأَلْفِ سَنَةٍ مِّمَّا تَعُدُّونَ ۝}$$

(الحج 47)

"And they urge you to hasten the punishment. But Allah will never fail in His promise. And indeed, a day with your Lord is like a thousand years of those which you count."

Surat Al-Haj, Ayah 47 [101].

92

The second aya is:

$$يُدَبِّرُ ٱلْأَمْرَ مِنَ ٱلسَّمَآءِ إِلَى ٱلْأَرْضِ ثُمَّ يَعْرُجُ إِلَيْهِ فِى يَوْمٍ كَانَ مِقْدَارُهُۥٓ أَلْفَ سَنَةٍ مِّمَّا تَعُدُّونَ ۝٥$$

(السجدة 5)

"He arranges (each) matter from the heaven to the earth; then it will ascend to Him in a Day, the extent of which is a thousand years of those which you count".

Surat Al Sajdah, Ayah 5 [102].

A third aya speaks of a day which is equivalent to fifty thousand years:

$$تَعْرُجُ ٱلْمَلَٰٓئِكَةُ وَٱلرُّوحُ إِلَيْهِ فِى يَوْمٍ كَانَ مِقْدَارُهُۥ خَمْسِينَ أَلْفَ سَنَةٍ ۝٤$$

(المعارج/4)

"The angels and the Spirit will ascend to Him during a Day the measure of which is fifty thousand years."

Surat Al Maarij, Ayah 4. [103].

Ali Unal in his annotated interpretation of the Quran further explains this concept of time in the context of the verses, and also in perspectives of astrophysics and the sociology of history. Attention is drawn to the relativity of time. A long period in the perspective of humans may be very short in the sight of God. God does not consider time in the same way that the human being does, in the sense that He is not constrained by the concepts of time or space. To this, interestingly, he adds: *"He is not contained by time or space, and His Wisdom that directs things and events considers each thing and event both as an individual entity in and as an indispensable part of the general fabric of creation and history. As each thing in the universe has an intrinsic relationship not only with every other thing individually, but also with the whole universe at the same time, so too is each event in human history interrelated with every other event individually and with the whole history. Human beings cannot grasp this relationship in its entire web; they cannot know the past perfectly, grasp the present completely, nor guess the future well. Besides, the wheel of both the universe and history does not revolve according to the desires of human beings. Secondly, a day for humanity is the time it takes the earth to make a single rotation around itself. The earth has another day, which consists of its revolution around the sun. This day lasts 365 days according to the reckoning of a day by humanity. So too does every other planet and all systems, like the solar system, have a day that is peculiar to each. This means that the concept of a day differs according to the planets and the systems."* [104]

On page 854 of his book Unal also mentions in his explanation of the verse in Surat As- Sajdah: *"The Quran uses the word day not only in the sense of a normal day, but also as time unit and period. While this verse mentions a day to be equivalent of 1,000 years by our reckoning, another verse mentions a day that measures 50,000 years (70:4). This shows that the concept of day is relative. The world does not consist only in our world or the visible universe. Rather there are worlds or dimensions within one another. Just as time or the length of a day is different in the world of dreams, so too is it also different in the world of spirit and imagination and that of immaterial forms, in other spiritual realms"*. [105]

The third word in the aya is دين deen. This word has several meanings including religion, law, habit and obedience. It also means recompense and reward. In 33 different published English translations of the Quran the different translators used for the translation of the word deen in this aya the following words in the following frequencies: (a) Judgement – 22 times; (b) Doom – 2 times; (c) Repayment – 2 times;

(d) Requital – 2 times; (e) Reckoning – 2 times; (f) Recompense– 2 times; (g) Resurrection – 1 time.

Yawm Ad-Deen is part of الآخرة Al-Akhirah i.e. of the Hereafter or Ending. To be accepted by Allah a person needs not only to believe in Allah and live righteously and do good in life, but also must believe in the Hereafter and اليوم الآخر Al-Yawm Al-Akher i.e. the Day of Judgement and Requital. The Quran states:

$$ وَمَنْ أَرَادَ ٱلْآخِرَةَ وَسَعَىٰ لَهَا سَعْيَهَا وَهُوَ مُؤْمِنٌ فَأُولَٰئِكَ كَانَ سَعْيُهُم مَّشْكُورًا ﴿١٩﴾ $$

الاسراء 19

"But whoever desires the Hereafter and exerts the effort due to it while he is a believer - it is those whose effort is ever appreciated (by Allah)".

Surat Al-Isra (The Assension), Ayah 19 [106].

The Quran also states:

$$ يُؤْمِنُونَ بِٱللَّهِ وَٱلْيَوْمِ ٱلْآخِرِ وَيَأْمُرُونَ بِٱلْمَعْرُوفِ وَيَنْهَوْنَ عَنِ ٱلْمُنكَرِ وَيُسَٰرِعُونَ فِي ٱلْخَيْرَٰتِ وَأُولَٰئِكَ مِنَ ٱلصَّٰلِحِينَ ﴿١١٤﴾ $$

(آل عمران 114)

"They believe in Allah and the Last Day, and they enjoin what is right and forbid what is wrong and hasten to good deeds. And those are among the righteous"

Surat Aal-Imran, Ayah 114 [107]

The Day of Judgement also has many other names referred to in the Holy Quran including; الآخرة *Al Akhirah* (The Ending) – Surat Al Baqarah 4:2; الحاقة *Al Haqqah* (The Righteous Coming) – Surat Al Haqqah 1,2,3:69; الساعة *Al Saa-ah* (The Hour) - Surat Al An-am 31:6; الصاخة *Al Sakhah* (The Deafening Wrath) - Surat Abasa; الطامة الكبرى *Al Tamat-Al-Kubra* (The Great Resurrection Event) - Surat Al Nazi-at 34:79; الغاشية *Al Ghashiyah* (The Enveloper) - Surat Al Ghashiyah 1:88; القارعة *Al Qariaah* (The Striker/The Pounder) - Surat Al Qaria'ah 1-3:101 and Surat Al Haqqah 4:69; الميعاد *Al Miyaad* (The Appointment) - Surat Al Qasas 85:28; الواقعة *Al Wakiaah* (The Event) - Surat Al Wakiaah 1:56; يوم البعث *Yawm Al Baath* (Day of Resurrection) - Surat Al Rum 56:30; يوم التغابن *Yawm Al Taghabun* (Day of Gathering) - Surat Al Taghabun 9:64; يوم التلاقي *Yawm Al Talaqi* (Day of Mutual Meeting – Resurrection) - Surat Ghafir 15:40; يوم الجمع *Yawm Al Jaamm* (Day of Assembly) - Surat Al Shurra 7:42; يوم الحسرة *Yawm Al Hassra* (Day of Grief- Regrets) - Surat Maryam 39:19; يوم الفصل *Yawm Al Fasal* (Day of Judgement) - Surat Al Saffat 21:37; يوم القيامة *Yawm Al Qiyaamah* (Day of Resurrection) - Surat Al Qiyaamah 1:75; يوم الوعيد *Yawm Al Waeed* (Day of Whereof Warning) - Surat Qaf 20:50.

Although all the names refer to the same Day, they highlight certain events or aspects that occur on that Day. For example, Yawm Al Qiyaamah is "The Day of Resurrection", which is one of the stages which mankind will go through. Al Wakiaah is "The Event", but in Al-Fatihah Allah (SWT) chooses "Yawm Ad-Deen" invoking an important dimension of that Day, which in fact is its climax and which is the ultimate purpose of that Day, which is Judgement, Requital and Recompense!

The phrase *Yawm Al-Deen* appears in the Quran 10 times in the following *suras*: Al-Fatihah 4:1; Al Hajar 35:15; Al Shuarra 82:26; Al Safat 20:37; Saad 78:38; Al Dhariyat 12:51; Al Wakiaa 56:56; Al Infithar 15, 17 & 18:82.

Abul Kalam Azad [108] states that Al Din, (or Al-Deen), comes from the Semitic languages used in the sense of requital and recompense. He defines Maalik Yawm Ad-Deen as *"He who is the dispenser of Justice on the Day of Requital"*. In his thesis he states: *"The Quran uses the term Al Din generally in the sense of requital. That is why it refers to the Day of Judgment as the Day of requital. It is so styled because the Quran attempts to point out that requital or justice is the inevitable result of one's own actions and not arbitrarily imposed as was the idea prevailing when the Quran was delivered. The old belief had been inspired by the absolutism or despotism of rulers, and a similitude entertained in respect of God suggesting that even as the absolute monarchs those Days, God could dispense reward or punishment as His whim suggested. It was why people in those Days propitiated the Deity by various forms of sacrifices. The idea was to humor Him up and keep His temper at the normal"*.

Azad states that the reward or punishment is the natural consequence and is consistent with the law of causation in operation in the universe. This therefore means that every action will have an inevitable reaction and good actions are rewarded and bad actions are punished. That is requital and recompense.

This is further explained in the following verses:

$$أَمْ حَسِبَ ٱلَّذِينَ ٱجْتَرَحُوا۟ ٱلسَّيِّـَٔاتِ أَن نَّجْعَلَهُمْ كَٱلَّذِينَ ءَامَنُوا۟ وَعَمِلُوا۟ ٱلصَّٰلِحَٰتِ سَوَآءً مَّحْيَاهُمْ وَمَمَاتُهُمْ سَآءَ مَا يَحْكُمُونَ ﴿٢١﴾$$

"Or do those who commit evils think We will make them like those who have believed and done righteous deeds – (make them) equal in their life and their death? Evil is that which they judge."

$$وَخَلَقَ اللَّهُ السَّمَوَاتِ وَالْأَرْضَ بِالْحَقِّ وَلِتُجْزَىٰ كُلُّ نَفْسٍ بِمَا كَسَبَتْ وَهُمْ لَا يُظْلَمُونَ ﴿٢٢﴾$$

(الجاثية21 و22)

[And Allah created the heavens and earth in truth and so that every soul may be recompensed for what it has earned, and they will not be wronged]

Surat Al-Jathiyah, Ayat 21-22 [109]

Sheikh Muhammad Abdoh [110] defined Al Deen as حساب "Hesab" or Recourse/Judgement also الجزاء "*Al Jazzaa*". The Lord (SWT) said that He will be the King/Master of the Day of Al Deen. Yet the Quran states that many will deny the coming of that Day:

$$كَلَّا بَلْ تُكَذِّبُونَ بِالدِّينِ ﴿٩﴾$$

(الانفطار 9)

"No! But you deny the Recompense."

Surat Al Infitar, Ayat 9 [111]

In another Translation by Daryabadi, 2001 translation [112] of the Meanings this verse reads *[No indeed! Aye! You deny the Requital!]*.

Sheikh Muhammad Abduh [113] went through a long discussion on the recourse of actions both good and bad, positive reward and negative outcomes, for all those who do well and bad respectively. He says that these outcomes in this life:

(a) Do not always necessarily compare to the action taken – be it good or bad and, therefore, man may not get the full reward he deserves for his actions or the right level of punishment for his bad and evil doings.

(b) When rewarded or punished in this life, this is done in seclusion or in front of a few persons and not the whole of humanity which would add to the honour of reward or the embarrassment of punishment etc.

(c) In fact, the recourse is so accurate and exact that Allah (SWT) says:

$$\text{فَمَن يَعْمَلْ مِثْقَالَ ذَرَّةٍ خَيْرًا يَرَهُ ۝}$$

$$\text{وَمَن يَعْمَلْ مِثْقَالَ ذَرَّةٍ شَرًّا يَرَهُ ۝}$$

(الزلزلة 7 و 8)

"So whoever does an atom's weight of good will see it".
"And whoever does an atom's weight of evil will see it"
Surat Az-Zalzalah, Ayat 8-9 [114].

This verse demonstrates the accuracy of requital and judgement although the Lord (SWT) does reward and punish also people in their lives on earth but in the Day of judgement all will be absolutely and accurately equalised.

The Quran also states:

$$\text{مَّنْ عَمِلَ صَالِحًا فَلِنَفْسِهِ ۖ وَمَنْ أَسَاءَ فَعَلَيْهَا ۗ وَمَا رَبُّكَ بِظَلَّامٍ لِّلْعَبِيدِ ۝}$$

(فصلت 41:46)

"Whoever does righteousness - it is for his (own) soul; and whoever does evil (does so) against it. And your Lord is not ever unjust to (His) servants.
Surat Fussilat, Ayah 46. [115]

Al-Fatihah

According to a *Hadith* of the Prophet (ﷺ):

إن الله كتب الحسنات والسيئات ثم بين ذلك فمن هم بحسنة فلم يعملها كتبها الله

له عنده حسنة كاملة فإن هو هم بها فعملها كتبها الله له عنده عشر حسنات إلى

سبع مائة ضعف إلى أضعاف كثيرة ومن هم هم بسيئة فلم يعملها كتبها الله له عنده

حسنة كاملة فإن هو هم بها فعملها كتبها الله له سيئة واحدة.

(رواه البخاري ومسلم)

"Allah has written down the good deeds and the bad ones. Then He explained it [by saying that] he who has intended a good deed and has not done it, Allah writes it down with Himself a full good deed, but if he has intended it and has done it, Allah writes it down with Himself as from ten good deeds to seven hundred times, or many times over. But if he has intended a bad deed and has not done it, Allah writes it down with Himself as a full good deed, but if he has intended it and has done it, Allah writes it down as one bad deed." (narrated by Al-Bukhari and Muslim. [116]

In one of the most blessed verses of the Quran which is full of mercy we read:

لَا يُكَلِّفُ ٱللَّهُ نَفْسًا إِلَّا وُسْعَهَا لَهَا مَا كَسَبَتْ وَعَلَيْهَا مَا
ٱكْتَسَبَتْ رَبَّنَا لَا تُؤَاخِذْنَا إِن نَّسِينَا أَوْ أَخْطَأْنَا رَبَّنَا وَلَا تَحْمِلْ
عَلَيْنَا إِصْرًا كَمَا حَمَلْتَهُ عَلَى ٱلَّذِينَ مِن قَبْلِنَا رَبَّنَا وَلَا تُحَمِّلْنَا
مَا لَا طَاقَةَ لَنَا بِهِ وَٱعْفُ عَنَّا وَٱغْفِرْ لَنَا وَٱرْحَمْنَا أَنتَ مَوْلَىٰنَا
فَٱنصُرْنَا عَلَى ٱلْقَوْمِ ٱلْكَافِرِينَ ﴿٢٨٦﴾

(البقرة 286)

"Allah does not charge a soul except (with that within) its capacity. It will have (the consequence of) what (good) it has gained, and it will bear (the consequence of) what (evil) it has earned. "Our Lord, do not impose blame upon us if we have forgotten or erred. Our Lord, and lay not upon us a burden like that which You laid upon those before us. Our Lord, and burden us not with that which we have no ability to bear. And pardon us; and forgive us; and have mercy upon us. You are our protector, so give us victory over the disbelieving people.""

Surat Al Baqarah (The Cow), Ayah 286 [117].

The Quran refers to the wider human belief in the existence of the higher being, a God and His creation of this whole universe in the very first instance. However, it also refers to the polytheists who whilst recognizing this fact failed to believe in the Hereafter.

Al Baghawi, interprets this following aya in explaining that: Oh Muhammed (ﷺ), when you ask them (i.e. the polytheists from your people) who then created you, they respond Allah, however, then they deny themselves salvation and His Mercy by not following His commandments and this amounts or leads to their delusion which they have effectively earned through their abstinence [118].

The following aya explains this:

$$وَلَئِن سَأَلْتَهُم مَّنْ خَلَقَهُمْ لَيَقُولُنَّ ٱللَّهُ فَأَنَّىٰ يُؤْفَكُونَ ۝٨٧$$

(الزخرف87)

"And if you asked them who created them, they would surely say, "Allah." So how are they deluded?"

Surat Az-Zukhruf, Ayah 87 [119]

To this end man would never reach that righteous level of behaviour in this world if he did not believe in the Hereafter. Only when he believes in this he will work hard and sacrifice much in order to ensure recompense in the permanent life in the Hereafter. Without this belief he will not ultimately manage his behaviours and actions.

Sheikh Muhammad Abduh [120] makes the important remark that because God is the Greatest and The Most Merciful He preceded the great verse Malik Yaum Al-Deen with "Al Rahman Al Raheem" to encourage mankind to follow His orders in the "enticement and dissuation" approach as in:

$$\text{۞ نَبِّئْ عِبَادِى أَنِّى أَنَا ٱلْغَفُورُ ٱلرَّحِيمُ ﴿٤٩﴾}$$

$$\text{وَأَنَّ عَذَابِى هُوَ ٱلْعَذَابُ ٱلْأَلِيمُ ﴿٥٠﴾}$$

(الحجر 49 و50)

"(O Muhammad), inform My servants that it is I who am the Forgiving, the Merciful"
And that it is My punishment which is the painful punishment"
Surat Al Hijr, Ayat 49-50 [121].

Here we also must mention the *Hadith* that informs us that one does not enter paradise because of his good deeds but by the mercy of Allah:

قال رسول الله صلى الله عليه وسلم لن ينجي أحدا منكم عمله قالوا ولا أنت يا

رسول الله قال ولا أنا إلا أن يتغمدني الله برحمة سددوا وقاربوا واغدوا وروحوا

وشيء من الدلجة والقصد القصد تبلغوا

(رواه البخاري)

Chapter 7: Maliki Yawm Ad-Deen

This *Hadith* means:

The Prophet (ﷺ) said: *"The deeds of anyone of you will not save you (from the (Hell) Fire)." They said, "Even you (will not be saved by your deeds), O Allah's Messenger (ﷺ)?" He said, "No, even I (will not be saved) unless and until Allah bestows His Mercy on me. Therefore, do good deeds properly, sincerely and moderately, and worship Allah in the forenoon and in the afternoon and during a part of the night, and always adopt a middle, moderate, regular course whereby you will reach your target (Paradise)." [Narrated by Bukhairi].* [122]

Nobody will enter Paradise, no matter how good he/she was, through his/her deeds. Good deeds will only be the means to acquire Allah's Mercy and Permission to enter Paradise.

Lings (2007) [123] offered in the *"Translations of Selected Verses"* two versions of the translation of Maalik Yawm Ad-Deen. The first is the Allen & Unwin (1983) text which talks of *"Master of the Day of Judgement"*. In the second they refer to unpublished material between 1938 and 2005 and offer *"Owner of the Day of Judgement"*.

As discussed, both the two readings: Malik and Maalik are acceptable. The meanings, although different, lead to the exact same interpretation. The Lord (SWT) will be the King and Master and Owner in the Day of Requital. As He ultimately owns time and space, He is the Master of its arrival and will reside as the Sovereign Master in that hour of judgement. It is not easy to make a single approximation translation here as both words in Arabic are acceptable; however, given this long discussion perhaps the best closest approximation would be **"Sovereign Master"**. Although many of the translations talk of Judgement, and although Yawm Ad-Deen is the Day of Judgement, perhaps a better translation could be Day of Requital and Recompense. As Day can be explained in terms of a specified period, the authors suggest a translation of the meaning of Maalik Yawm Ad-Deen as: ***"Sovereign Master of the Day of Recompense"***.

Chapter 8

إِيَّاكَ نَعْبُدُ وإِيَّاكَ نَسْتَعِينُ

Iyaka Na'budu wa Iyaka Nasta'een

In the three ayas before this aya and also in the Basmalah at the beginning of Al-Fatihah, Allah is spoken of in the third person, but in this aya "Iyaka Na'budu wa Iyaka Nasta'een" Allah is addressed in the second person. The change from first to second persons or second to third persons, etc is not unusual in Arabic literature and poetry. It is classically known in Arabic grammar as *iltifat* (which means looking from one direction to another). It is supposed to add colour to the style and it helps keep the attention of the reader or listener. Unal (2007) suggested that the servant of Allah has addressed Him in the third person until the 4th verse, but has climbed the ladder to rise to His Presence and there attain the dignity of addressing Him in the second person [124].

In the previous ayas of Al-Fatihah the verses start in the Name of Allah and praise Him and declare that He is the most benificient and in His hands is the Day of Judgement. Now the verse addresses Allah directly. It has two parts: the first states that "You alone we worship", and the second that "You alone we ask for help". Some scolars in previous eras stated that Al-Fatihah is the essence (or secret) of the Quran, and the essence of Al-Fatihah is this particular verse.

For instance the Sheikh of Islam Ibn Taymiyyah in his book "The Clear Way of the Prophet's Sunna" related that Al-Hasan Al-Basri, may Allah rest his soul, said that Allah has sent down one hundred and four books, whose secret (or essence) has been condensed in four, and He gathered the secret of the the four in the Quran, and the secret of the Quran in Al-Fatihah, and the secret of Al-Fatihah in these two "words" (i.e. sentences) 'You alone we worship, and You alone we ask for help', and therefore, he repeated them in more than one place in the Quran such as *"so worship Him and rely upon Him"*, Surat Hood, Ayah123. [125]

قال شيخ الإسلام ابن تيمية في منهاج السنة النبوية: وقد روي عن الحسن البصري رحمه الله أن الله أنزل مائة كتاب وأربعة كتب جمع سرها في الأربعة وجمع سر الأربعة في القرآن وجمع سر القرآن في الفاتحة وجمع سر الفاتحة في هاتين الكلمتين إياك نعبد وإياك نستعين. ولهذا ثناها الله في كتابه في غير موضع من القرآن كقوله:"فَاعْبُدْهُ وَتَوَكَّلْ عَلَيْهِ" (هود/123).

The first part of this aya is a repudiation of *shirk* (or polytheism) and the second part is a repudiation that any but Allah has the true power and the might and ability to aid.

Iyaka na'budu:

The word *Iyaka* means you, but it is in the objective case. Normally the object in an Arabic sentence comes after the verb and also normally after the subject. Because it is placed at the beginning of the sentence the stress is placed on it, and it conveys the meaning of exclusivity of you alone and no one else.

The word *na'budu* means we worship. The past tense singular is *a'bada* meaning he or she worshiped. The noun *i'badah* means worshipping, which includes the meaning of obedience with humility and submission. The noun *u'boodiyah* means worshipping and it also means slavery. The noun *a'bd* means either worshipper or slave. The plural of *a'bd* is *i'bad* which usually means worshippers and is also *a'beed* which means slaves but could also mean worshippers. In Arabic a road flattened by frequent use or paved (with stones, tarmac, etc.) is called *tareeq* (i.e. road) *mua'bbad* (i.e. flattened or paved). Similarly a tamed camel is called *ba'eer* (i.e. camel) *mua'bbad* (i.e. tamed). The use of *na'budu* i.e. we worship (in the plural) apparently signifies that the act of worship is best done in *jama'a* i.e. a group as happens in the five ordained prayers during a day which are according to one *hadith* 27 times better when performed in a group than when performed by a person by himself.

The contemporary Islamic scholar and Quran interpreter Sheikh Muhammad Mutawali Ash-Sha'rawi explained the difference between *i'bad* and *a'beed*. He stated that all humans have no choice in so many aspects of their lives such as their heart beats, their colour and their looks, etc and this is the *i'badah* of non-choice dictated by Allah's force. But Allah has allowed humans and the *jinn* the *i'badah* of choice or love, where they can believe in Allah or not, and can obey Him or not. Those who achieve the *i'badah* of love or choice become *i'bad*. But those who do not choose to believe and obey, are merely *a'beed*. [126]. The following ayas of the Quran say:

وَعِبَادُ ٱلرَّحْمَٰنِ ٱلَّذِينَ يَمْشُونَ عَلَى ٱلْأَرْضِ هَوْنًا وَإِذَا خَاطَبَهُمُ ٱلْجَٰهِلُونَ قَالُوا۟ سَلَٰمًا ۝٦٣

وَٱلَّذِينَ يَبِيتُونَ لِرَبِّهِمْ سُجَّدًا وَقِيَٰمًا ۝٦٤

وَٱلَّذِينَ يَقُولُونَ رَبَّنَا ٱصْرِفْ عَنَّا عَذَابَ جَهَنَّمَ إِنَّ عَذَابَهَا كَانَ غَرَامًا ۝٦٥

(الفرقان 63-65)

"And the servants of Ar-Rahman (Allah) Most Gracious are those who walk on the earth in humility, and when the ignorant address them, they say, "Peace!"."

"Those who spend the night in adoration of their Lord prostrate and standing"

[Those who say: "Our Lord! avert from us the Wrath of Hell, for its Wrath is indeed an affliction grievous."]

Surat Al Furqan (The Criterian), Ayat 63-65 [127]

The word i'bad appears in several other verses such as:

وَإِذَا سَأَلَكَ عِبَادِى عَنِّى فَإِنِّى قَرِيبٌ أُجِيبُ دَعْوَةَ ٱلدَّاعِ إِذَا دَعَانِ فَلْيَسْتَجِيبُوا لِى وَلْيُؤْمِنُوا بِى لَعَلَّهُمْ يَرْشُدُونَ ﴿١٨٦﴾

(البقرة/186)

"And when My servants ask you, concerning Me - indeed I am near. I respond to the invocation of the supplicant when he calls upon Me. So let them respond to Me (by obedience) and believe in Me that they may be (rightly) guided."

Surat Al Baqarah (The Cow), Ayah 186 [128]

يَـٰعِبَادِ لَا خَوْفٌ عَلَيْكُمُ ٱلْيَوْمَ وَلَا أَنتُمْ تَحْزَنُونَ ﴿٦٨﴾

(الزخرف/68)

[(To whom Allah will say), "O My servants, no fear will there be concerning you this Day, nor will you grieve"]

Surat Az-Zukhruf, Ayah 68 [129]

قَالَ فَبِعِزَّتِكَ لَأُغْوِيَنَّهُمْ أَجْمَعِينَ ﴿٨٢﴾

"(Iblees) said, "By your might, I will surely mislead them all"

إِلَّا عِبَادَكَ مِنْهُمُ ٱلْمُخْلَصِينَ ۝

(ص 82 و83)

"Except, among them, Your chosen servants."

Surat Sa'ad, Ayah 82-83 [130]

In another aya the Quran describes those who have erred extensively as *i'bad* but perhaps if they do not despair of Allah's mercy:

۞ قُلْ يَٰعِبَادِيَ ٱلَّذِينَ أَسْرَفُوا۟ عَلَىٰٓ أَنفُسِهِمْ لَا تَقْنَطُوا۟ مِن رَّحْمَةِ ٱللَّهِ إِنَّ ٱللَّهَ يَغْفِرُ ٱلذُّنُوبَ جَمِيعًا إِنَّهُۥ هُوَ ٱلْغَفُورُ ٱلرَّحِيمُ ۝

(الزمر/53)

"Say, "O My servants who have transgressed against themselves [by sinning], do not despair of the mercy of Allah. Indeed, Allah forgives all sins. Indeed, it is He who is the Forgiving, the Merciful."

Surat Az-Zumar, Ayah 53 [131]

In another aya the Quran describes the servants as *ibad* not *abeed*, but according to some interpreters like Al-Sha'rawi this is in the hereafter when all human beings become believers in Allah and loose the choice to be unbelievers:

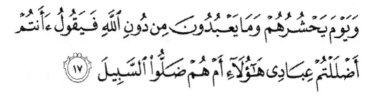

وَيَوْمَ يَحْشُرُهُمْ وَمَا يَعْبُدُونَ مِن دُونِ ٱللَّهِ فَيَقُولُ ءَأَنتُمْ أَضْلَلْتُمْ عِبَادِى هَٰٓؤُلَآءِ أَمْ هُمْ ضَلُّوا۟ ٱلسَّبِيلَ ۝

(الفرقان: 17)

"And (mention) the Day He will gather them and that which they worship besides Allah and will say, "Did you mislead these, My servants, or did they (themselves) stray from the way?""
Surat Al-Furqan (The Criterian), Ayah 17 [132]

But when Allah speaks of human beings at large i.e. both believers and non-believers together, He normally calls them *a'beed,* those who serve Him, for instance in the following aya which appears in two *suras:*

(آل عمران/182، الأنفال/51)

"That is for what your hands have put forth (of evil) and because Allah is not ever unjust to His servants.""
Surat Anfal 51 & Surat Aal-Imran, Ayah 182. [133]

For a Muslim the purpose of life is clearly and directly stated in the Quran:

وَمَا خَلَقْتُ الْجِنَّ وَالْإِنسَ إِلَّا لِيَعْبُدُونِ ﴿٥٦﴾

(الذاريات/56)

"And I did not create the jinn and mankind except to worship Me."
Surat Al Dharriyat, Ayah 56 [134]

Thus Allah has created both the jinn and human beings to worship Him.

The Quran also states:

أَفَحَسِبْتُمْ أَنَّمَا خَلَقْنَاكُمْ عَبَثًا وَأَنَّكُمْ إِلَيْنَا لَا تُرْجَعُونَ ﴿١١٥﴾

(المؤمنون/115)

"Did ye then think that We had created you in jest (without purpose), and that ye would not be brought back to Us (for account)?"

Surat Al Mu'minon, Ayah 115. [135].

The Quran also states:

$$\text{۞ وَإِلَىٰ ثَمُودَ أَخَاهُمْ صَـٰلِحًا ۚ قَالَ يَـٰقَوْمِ ٱعْبُدُوا۟ ٱللَّهَ مَا لَكُم مِّنْ إِلَـٰهٍ}$$

$$\text{غَيْرُهُۥ ۖ هُوَ أَنشَأَكُم مِّنَ ٱلْأَرْضِ وَٱسْتَعْمَرَكُمْ فِيهَا فَٱسْتَغْفِرُوهُ ثُمَّ تُوبُوٓا۟ إِلَيْهِ ۚ}$$

$$\text{إِنَّ رَبِّى قَرِيبٌ مُّجِيبٌ ﴿١١﴾}$$

(هود/61)

"And to Thamud (We sent) their brother Salih. He said, "O my people, worship Allah; you have no deity other than Him. He has produced you from the earth and settled you in it, so ask forgiveness of Him and then repent to Him. Indeed, my Lord is near and responsive.""

Surat Hud, Ayah 61 [136]

These Ayas tell us that Allah has created us to worship Him. He created us from the earth and wants us to develop this earth that he gave to us to the better, together with the rest of mankind, always bearing Allah in our minds and realizing that He is so near. The Quran states:

$$\text{وَلَقَدْ خَلَقْنَا ٱلْإِنسَـٰنَ وَنَعْلَمُ مَا تُوَسْوِسُ بِهِۦ نَفْسُهُۥ ۖ وَنَحْنُ أَقْرَبُ إِلَيْهِ مِنْ}$$

$$\text{حَبْلِ ٱلْوَرِيدِ ﴿١٦﴾}$$

(ق/16)

"It was We Who created man, and We know what dark suggestions his soul makes to him: for We are nearer to him than (his) jugular vein"

Surat Qaf, Ayah 16. [137].

Worshipping Allah entails the belief that he is the one and only God and that He has no partners, and He is neither begotten, nor begets. Surat Al-Ikhlas states:

$$ قُلْ هُوَ ٱللَّهُ أَحَدٌ ۝١ $$

$$ ٱللَّهُ ٱلصَّمَدُ ۝٢ $$

$$ لَمْ يَلِدْ وَلَمْ يُولَدْ ۝٣ $$

$$ وَلَمْ يَكُن لَّهُۥ كُفُوًا أَحَدٌۢ ۝٤ $$

"Say, "He is Allah, (who is) One,'
"Allah, the Eternal Refuge."
"He neither begets nor is born (begotten),"
"Nor is there to Him any equivalent.""

Surat Al Iklas, Ayat 1-4 [138]

The oneness of Allah is argued in the following aya:

$$ لَوْ كَانَ فِيهِمَآ ءَالِهَةٌ إِلَّا ٱللَّهُ لَفَسَدَتَا فَسُبْحَٰنَ ٱللَّهِ رَبِّ ٱلْعَرْشِ عَمَّا يَصِفُونَ ۝٢٢ $$

الأنبياء 22/

"Had there been within the heavens and earth gods besides Allah, they both would have been ruined. So exalted is Allah, Lord of the Throne, above what they describe"

Surat Al-Anbya, Ayah 22. [139].

But the bedrock of worship, as explained by Ibn Al-Qayyim in his book Madarej As-Salikeen, is the love of Allah, and that all love should be to Allah and to Him alone. One should not love anyone or anything else with Allah, but should love others such as the messengers, prophets, angels, and the devoted believers for the sake of Allah. The Quran clearly states:

وَمِنَ ٱلنَّاسِ مَن يَتَّخِذُ مِن دُونِ ٱللَّهِ أَندَادًا يُحِبُّونَهُمْ كَحُبِّ ٱللَّهِ ۖ وَٱلَّذِينَ ءَامَنُوٓاْ أَشَدُّ حُبًّا لِّلَّهِ ۗ وَلَوْ يَرَى ٱلَّذِينَ ظَلَمُوٓاْ إِذْ يَرَوْنَ ٱلْعَذَابَ أَنَّ ٱلْقُوَّةَ لِلَّهِ جَمِيعًا وَأَنَّ ٱللَّهَ شَدِيدُ ٱلْعَذَابِ ﴿١٦٥﴾

البقرة/165

"And (yet), among the people are those who take other than Allah as equals [to Him]. They love them as they (should) love Allah. But those who believe are stronger in love for Allah. And if only they who have wronged would consider (that) when they see the punishment, (they will be certain) that all power belongs to Allah and that Allah is severe in punishment"

Surat Al Baqarah (The Cow), Ayah 165 [140]

The Quran states clearly that Allah will not forgive *shirk* or polytheism or association of other gods with Allah:

إِنَّ ٱللَّهَ لَا يَغْفِرُ أَن يُشْرَكَ بِهِۦ وَيَغْفِرُ مَا دُونَ ذَٰلِكَ لِمَن يَشَآءُ ۚ وَمَن يُشْرِكْ بِٱللَّهِ فَقَدِ ٱفْتَرَىٰٓ إِثْمًا عَظِيمًا ﴿٤٨﴾

النساء/48

"Indeed, Allah does not forgive association with Him, but He forgives what is less than that for whom He wills. And he who associates others with Allah has certainly fabricated a tremendous sin."

Surat Al Nisa (Women), Ayah 48 [141]

إِنَّ ٱللَّهَ لَا يَغْفِرُ أَن يُشْرَكَ بِهِۦ وَيَغْفِرُ مَا دُونَ ذَٰلِكَ لِمَن يَشَآءُ وَمَن يُشْرِكْ بِٱللَّهِ فَقَدْ ضَلَّ ضَلَٰلًا بَعِيدًا ﴿١١٦﴾

النساء/ 116

"Indeed, Allah does not forgive association with Him, but He forgives what is less than that for whom He wills. And he who associates others with Allah has certainly gone far astray."

Surat Al Nisa (Women), Ayah 116 [142]

In another aya the Quran states that disbelievers whether they are people of the scripture or polytheists, will abide eternally in Hell:

إِنَّ ٱلَّذِينَ كَفَرُوا۟ مِنْ أَهْلِ ٱلْكِتَٰبِ وَٱلْمُشْرِكِينَ فِى نَارِ جَهَنَّمَ خَٰلِدِينَ فِيهَآ أُو۟لَٰٓئِكَ هُمْ شَرُّ ٱلْبَرِيَّةِ ﴿٦﴾

(البينة/6)

"Indeed, they who disbelieved among the People of the Scripture and the polytheists will be in the fire of Hell, abiding eternally therein. Those are the worst of creatures."

Surat Al Bayyinah, Ayah 6 [143]

Allah loves those who love him, and to know how to love Allah one must follow His instructions and avoid what He has forbidden, i.e. follow the guidance of the Prophet. The Quran states:

قُلْ إِن كُنتُمْ تُحِبُّونَ اللَّهَ فَاتَّبِعُونِي يُحْبِبْكُمُ اللَّهُ وَيَغْفِرْ لَكُمْ ذُنُوبَكُمْ وَاللَّهُ غَفُورٌ رَّحِيمٌ ﴿٣١﴾

(آل عمران/31)

"Say, (O Muhammad), "If you should love Allah, then follow me, (so) Allah will love you and forgive you your sins. And Allah is Forgiving and Merciful.""

Surat Aal-Imran, Ayah 31 [144]

The Quran tells us clearly that one should love Allah more than one loves himself, his kin or anyone else. He should also love the Prophet of Allah more than himself or anyone else:

قُلْ إِن كَانَ ءَابَآؤُكُمْ وَأَبْنَآؤُكُمْ وَإِخْوَٰنُكُمْ وَأَزْوَٰجُكُمْ وَعَشِيرَتُكُمْ وَأَمْوَٰلٌ اقْتَرَفْتُمُوهَا وَتِجَٰرَةٌ تَخْشَوْنَ كَسَادَهَا وَمَسَٰكِنُ تَرْضَوْنَهَآ أَحَبَّ إِلَيْكُم مِّنَ اللَّهِ وَرَسُولِهِ وَجِهَادٍ فِي سَبِيلِهِ فَتَرَبَّصُوا حَتَّىٰ يَأْتِيَ اللَّهُ بِأَمْرِهِ وَاللَّهُ لَا يَهْدِي الْقَوْمَ الْفَٰسِقِينَ ﴿٢٤﴾

(التوبة/24)

"Say, (O Muhammad), "If your fathers, your sons, your brothers, your wives, your relatives, wealth which you have obtained, commerce wherein you fear decline, and dwellings with which you are pleased are more beloved to you than Allah and His Messenger and jihad in His cause, then wait until Allah executes

His command. And Allah does not guide the defiantly disobedient people.""

Surat Al Tawbah, Ayah 24 [145]

The message of Islam is a message of love. The *hadith* states:

لا يؤمن أحدكم حتى يحب لأخيه ما يحب لنفسه (صحيح البخاري)

"None of you [truly] believes until he loves for his brother that which he loves for himself." (Narrated by Al-Bukhari) [146]

I'bada then is not just performing the obligatory and optional or voluntary *i'badat such as* prayers, fasting, zakat, haj, jihad and helping others. It is not just staying in mosques to pray and glorify Allah. It is rather a way of life that includes not only the actions of the body, but also the actions of the tongue such as glorifying Allah and defending Him, and making *da'wa* (i.e. spreading the message), and defending justice.

The Prophet (ﷺ) said, *"Convey from me even an Aya of the Qur'an.."* [147]

قال النبي صلى الله عليه وسلم: "بلغوا عني ولو آية.." (رواه البخاري)

The Quran states clearly that it is the duty of Muslims to ask people to do good and avoid wrong doing:

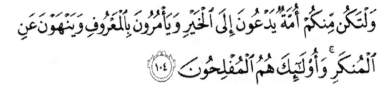

آل عمران اية 104

[And let there be (arising) from you a nation inviting to (all that is) good, enjoining what is right and forbidding what is wrong, and those will be the successful.]

Surat Aal-Imran, Ayah 104 [148]

But *ibadah* also includes the actions of the heart and above all things the love of Allah, and other actions of the heart such as the love of the prophets and angels and followers of the faith, and all those that Allah wants us to love.

Wa Iyaka nasta'een:

In chapter 2, about the importance of Al-Fatihah, we stated the *hadith* related by Muslim, part of which says *"And when he says: Iyyaka na'budu wa iyyaka nasta'een, He says: This is between Me and My servant, and My servant shall have what he has asked for."*

This is because in the first half of the verse the servant is saying to Allah that we worship Him alone and in the second half that we ask for help from Him alone. Although we need the help of Allah to be able to worship Him, the worship part of the verse comes before the part of asking for help, because the worship is a mean to the seeking of help. In any case it is obvious that the servant cannot worship Allah without His help. Moreover, worshipping includes asking for help, whereas asking for help does not necessarily include worshipping, because one can ask for help to do something which is not considered good.

The verse repeats the word "Iyyaka", i.e. You alone, because it is more eloquent (at least in the Arabic language) in this kind of sentence construction to repeat it with each verb. i.e. it is more eloquent in Arabic to say it as it actually stands, than to say "You alone we worship and ask for help".

Regarding asking for help there is a well-known hadith in which the Prophet (ﷺ) says to the young Ibn Abbas:

(يَا غُلَامُ, إِنِّي أُعَلِّمُكَ كَلِمَاتٍ: احْفَظِ اللَّهَ يَحْفَظْكَ, احْفَظِ اللَّهَ تَجِدْهُ تُجَاهَكَ, إِذَا

سَأَلْتَ فَاسْأَلِ اللَّهَ, وَإِذَا اسْتَعَنْتَ فَاسْتَعِنْ بِاللَّهِ, وَاعْلَمْ أَنَّ الْأُمَّةَ لَوِ اجْتَمَعَتْ عَلَى أَنْ

يَنْفَعُوكَ بِشَيْءٍ لَمْ يَنْفَعُوكَ إِلَّا بِشَيْءٍ قَدْ كَتَبَهُ اللَّهُ لَكَ, وَلَوِ اجْتَمَعُوا عَلَى أَنْ يَضُرُّوكَ

بِشَيْءٍ لَمْ يَضُرُّوكَ إِلَّا بِشَيْءٍ قَدْ كَتَبَهُ اللَّهُ عَلَيْكَ, رُفِعَتِ الْأَقْلَامُ وَجَفَّتِ الصُّحُفُ)

(رواه الترمذي)

i.e. "Young man, I shall teach you some words [of advice]: Be mindful of Allah, and Allah will protect you. Be mindful of Allah and you will find Him in front of you. If you ask, ask of Allah; if you seek help, seek help of Allah. Know that if the Nation were to gather together to benefit you with anything, it would benefit you only with something that Allah had already prescribed for you, and that if they gather together to harm you with anything, they would harm you only with something Allah had already prescribed for you. The pens have been lifted and the pages have dried." (Narrated by At-Tirmidhi) [149].

The person asking for help usually asks for it from someone more powerful, or capable or richer. He usually feels subdued when asking for it. But when he seeks the help from Allah, a true Muslim feels happy and honoured to be subdued in front of the Creator.

It is, however, acceptable to ask for help from others than Allah, provided help is sought from one who is living and probably has the ability to help. On the other hand, it is forbidden in Islam to ask for help from one who cannot deliver it, such as a dead saint, a grave, or an idol as this may amount to polytheism and associating the created with the Creator, which is the greatest sin in Islam.

In conclusion, we suggest the aya discussed in this chapter to be translated as follows: **"It is You (and You) alone we worship and You (and You) alone that we ask for help"**.

Chapter 9

اهْدِنَا الصِّرَاطَ الْمُسْتَقِيمَ

Ihdina As-Sirat Al-Mustaqeem

Al-Ghazali in his well-known book the classic "Ihya' Uloom ad-Deen" states that this verse which means "guide us to the right path" is a request and a prayer, and is the brain (i.e. core) of worship. It alerts the need in human beings to beseech Allah, which is the soul of worship, and alerts to their need for guidance.

The first word of the verse is اهدنا *ihdina* which means guide us or direct us, i.e. inspire us to know.

In Surat Al-Balad the Quran states:

أَلَمْ نَجْعَل لَّهُ عَيْنَيْنِ ﴿٨﴾

وَلِسَانًا وَشَفَتَيْنِ ﴿٩﴾

وَهَدَيْنَاهُ النَّجْدَيْنِ ﴿١٠﴾

البلد10-8

"Have We not made for him two eyes?"
"And a tongue and two lips?"
"And have shown him the two ways?"

Surat Al Balad, Ayat 8-10. [150].

118

These verses mean that Allah has equipped every person with eyes to see and a tongue and two lips to speak and has guided him and built into him the ability to distinguish the two paths of good and evil.

In Surat Al-Kahf the Quran states:

وَتَرَى ٱلشَّمْسَ إِذَا طَلَعَت تَّزَوَرُ عَن كَهْفِهِمْ ذَاتَ ٱلْيَمِينِ وَإِذَا غَرَبَت تَّقْرِضُهُمْ ذَاتَ ٱلشِّمَالِ وَهُمْ فِي فَجْوَةٍ مِّنْهُ ذَلِكَ مِنْ ءَايَتِ ٱللَّهِ مَن يَهْدِ ٱللَّهُ فَهُوَ ٱلْمُهْتَدِ وَمَن يُضْلِلْ فَلَن تَجِدَ لَهُ وَلِيًّا مُّرْشِدًا ۝

(الكهف/17)

"And (had you been present), you would see the sun when it rose, inclining away from their cave on the right, and when it set, passing away from them on the left, while they were (laying) within an open space thereof. That was from the signs of Allah. He whom Allah guides is the [rightly] guided, but he whom He leaves astray - never will you find for him a protecting guide."
Surat Al Kahf (The Cave), Ayat 17. [151].

Another aya states:

فَرِيقًا هَدَى وَفَرِيقًا حَقَّ عَلَيْهِمُ ٱلضَّلَلَةُ إِنَّهُمُ ٱتَّخَذُواْ ٱلشَّيَطِينَ أَوْلِيَآءَ مِن دُونِ ٱللَّهِ وَيَحْسَبُونَ أَنَّهُم مُّهْتَدُونَ ۝

(الأعراف/30)

"A group (of you) He guided, and a group deserved (to be in) error. Indeed, they had taken the devils as allies instead of Allah while they thought that they were guided"
Surat Al-A'araf, Ayah 30 [152].

Allah guides those who strive to follow the right path. In another aya the Quran states:

$$\text{وَٱلَّذِينَ جَٰهَدُواْ فِينَا لَنَهْدِيَنَّهُمْ سُبُلَنَاۚ وَإِنَّ ٱللَّهَ لَمَعَ ٱلْمُحْسِنِينَ ﴿٦٩﴾}$$

(العنكبوت/69)

"And those who strive for Us (i.e. in Our cause) - We will surely guide them to Our ways. And indeed, Allah is with the doers of good."

Surat Al-Ankaboot (The Spider), Ayah 69. [153]

In another aya the Quran says:

$$\text{إِنَّكَ لَا تَهْدِى مَنْ أَحْبَبْتَ وَلَٰكِنَّ ٱللَّهَ يَهْدِى مَن يَشَآءُۚ وَهُوَ أَعْلَمُ بِٱلْمُهْتَدِينَ ﴿٥٦﴾}$$

((القصص/56

"Indeed, (O Muhammad), you do not guide whom you like, but Allah guides whom He wills. And He is most knowing of the (rightly) guided."

Surat Al-Qasas, Ayah, 56. [154].

Interestingly this aya was addressed to the Prophet (ﷺ) when he was not able to convince his beloved uncle Abdul Muttaleb to embrace Islam until the moment the uncle passed away, although the uncle gave his nephew the Prophet (ﷺ) much needed protection against his polytheist tribe Quraish to spread the message of Islam but guidance is in the hands of Allah and no one else.

In this aya the guidance referred to is the "guidance of successful choice" that only if accepted and followed results in success. But of course, the Prophet (ﷺ) has been given by Allah the ability to indicate to believers and non-believers alike the right path and choice, i.e. he has been given the "guidance of illumination" that indicates the right path and choice but the final decision to accept that guidance rests fully with the person receiving that guidance.

The Quran states:

وَكَذَلِكَ أَوْحَيْنَا إِلَيْكَ رُوحًا مِّنْ أَمْرِنَا مَا كُنتَ تَدْرِى مَا ٱلْكِتَبُ وَلَا ٱلْإِيمَنُ وَلَكِن جَعَلْنَهُ نُورًا نَّهْدِى بِهِۦ مَن نَّشَآءُ مِنْ عِبَادِنَا وَإِنَّكَ لَتَهْدِىٓ إِلَىٰ صِرَطٍ مُّسْتَقِيمٍ ۝

(الشورى/52)

"And thus We have revealed to you an inspiration of Our command. You did not know what is the Book or (what is) faith, but We have made it a light by which We guide whom We will of Our servants. And indeed, (O Muhammad), you guide to a straight path"
Surat Ash-Shuraa, Ayah 52. [155].

The second word of the aya is *as-sirat* which means the path or road or way. Most of the standard recitations of the Quran recite as الصراط i.e. with the Arabic letter *sad* but some recite it as السراط with the Arabic letter *seen*. This is in conformity with the pronounciation of Quraish, the tribe of the Prophet (ﷺ) who used to pronounce a *sad* in place of the *seen*. It is also pronounced in some recitations as الزراط i.e. with the Arabic letter *zaai*. This is the way it was recited by tribes of Bani Udrah and Bani Kalb.

The noun *sirat* comes from the verb *sarata* which means swallowed. This is because it is as if a road swallows those who walk on it. There are other synonyms to sirat such as طريق *tareeq* i.e. road and سبيل *sabeel* i.e. way, but there are fine differences between them. For instance, according to the classic Arabic linguist and literary expert

Abu Hilal Al-Askari who died around 411-420 Hijri, a *sirat* is an easy road whereas a *tareeq* may or may not be easy.

The Quran states in one of its ayas:

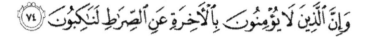

(المؤمنون/74)

"But indeed, those who do not believe in the Hereafter are deviating from the path."

Surat Al-Mu'minun, Ayah74 [156].

The last word of the aya is المستقيم i.e. al-mustaqeem which means the straight (and unbent or untwisted). So what is the straight path or road of Allah? We know from the above aya that those who do not believe in the hereafter are not on the right straight path.

Ali bin Abi Taleb (MABPWH), the 4th Calif or Khalifah said that the Prophet (ﷺ) said that as-sirat al-mustaqeem is the Book of Allah i.e. the Quran, in a hadith related by Ahmed and at-Tirmidhi.

إِنَّ اللَّهَ ضَرَبَ مَثَلاً صِرَاطًا مُسْتَقِيمًا عَلَى كَنَفِي الصِّرَاطِ دَارَانِ لَهُمَا أَبْوَابٌ مُفَتَّحَةٌ عَلَى الأَبْوَابِ سُتُورٌ وَدَاعٍ يَدْعُو عَلَى رَأْسِ الصِّرَاطِ وَدَاعٍ يَدْعُو فَوْقَهُ:)وَاللَّهُ يَدْعُو إِلَى دَارِ السَّلَامِ وَيَهْدِي مَنْ يَشَاءُ إِلَى صِرَاطٍ مُسْتَقِيمٍ(وَالأَبْوَابُ الَّتِي عَلَى كَنَفِي الصِّرَاطِ حُدُودُ اللَّهِ فَلاَ يَقَعُ أَحَدٌ فِي حُدُودِ اللَّهِ حَتَّى يُكْشَفَ السِّتْرُ وَالَّذِي يَدْعُو مِنْ فَوْقِهِ وَاعِظُ رَبِّهِ "

Narrated An-Nawwas bin Sam'an Al-Kilabi: that the Messenger of Allah (ﷺ) said: *"Indeed Allah has made a parable of the straight path: At the sides of the path there are walls with open doors, each door having a curtain. There is a caller at the head of the path calling, and a caller above it calling. And Allah invites to the abode of peace and guides whomever He wills to the straight path. The doors which are on the* sides of the path are the Hudud (legal limitations or sacrosancts) of Allah; no one breaches the Hudud of Allah except that curtain is lifted, and the one calling from above it is the preacher of his Lord." [157]. The preacher in the heart seems to be the conscience.

A Muslim repeats this aya at least 17 times a day if he performs only the prescribed prayers, and more times if he performs additional voluntary prayers. A Muslim needs to keep reminding himself of the need to stay on the right path because the Devil keeps trying to make him go astray. The hadith says:

"إِنَّ الشَّيْطَانَ يَجْرِي مِنْ الْإِنْسَانِ مَجْرَى الدَّمِ" (سنن أبي داود)

i.e. *"The devil runs in a human being like his blood"* (Narrated by Abu Dawud) [158].

Abu Bakr as-Siddiq (MABPWH), the 1st Caliph used to read the following aya in the 3rd rakka of every maghreb (sunset) prayer to remind himself to stay on the right path. He read this quietly to himself apparently as a beseeching rather than prayer recitation. This is narrated by Malek in a hadith in his Muwatta.

رَبَّنَا لَا تُزِغْ قُلُوبَنَا بَعْدَ إِذْ هَدَيْتَنَا وَهَبْ لَنَا مِن لَّدُنكَ رَحْمَةً إِنَّكَ أَنتَ الْوَهَّابُ ﴿٨﴾

آل عمران/8

[(Who say), "Our Lord, let not our hearts deviate after You have guided us and grant us from Yourself mercy. Indeed, You are the Bestower]

Surat Aal-Imran, 8 [159]

There is a well-known *hadith* which says:

"إن الحلال بين، وإن الحرام بين، وبينهما مشتبهات لا يعلمهن كثير من الناس، فمن اتقى الشبهات، استبرأ لدينه وعرضه، ومن وقع فى الشبهات، وقع فى الحرام، كالراعى يرعى حول الحمى يوشك أن يرتع فيه ألا وإن لكل ملك حمى، ألا وإن حمى الله محارمه، ألا وإن فى الجسد مضغة إذا صلحت صلح الجسد كله، وإذا فسدت فسد الجسد كله: ألا وهى القلب" ((متفق عليه. ورویاه من طرق بألفاظ متقاربة))

i.e. "What is lawful is clear and what is unlawful is clear, but between them are certain doubtful things which many people do not know. So he who guards against doubtful things keeps his religion and his honour blameless. But he who falls into doubtful things falls into that which is unlawful, just as a shepherd who grazes his cattle in the vicinity of a pasture declared prohibited (by the king); he is likely to stray into the pasture. Mind you, every king has a protected pasture and Allah's involved limits is that which He has declared unlawful. Verily, there is a piece of flesh in the body, if it is healthy, the whole body is healthy, and if it is corrupt, the whole body is corrupt. Verily, it is the heart." (Narrated by Al-Bukhari & Muslim) [160]

Another hadith says:

حفت الجنة بالمكاره وحفت النار بالشهوات (رواه مسلم وآخرون)

i.e. *"The Paradise is surrounded by hardships and the Hell-Fire is surrounded by temptations"* (Narrated by Muslim and others). [161].

The *sirat* in Al-Fatihah is related to our present life, and is different from the *sirat* in a *hadith* related by the narrator Muslim, which is related to the hereafter. That *sirat* in that *hadith* is a bridge over Hell which is thinner than a hair and sharper than the edge of the sword. The Prophet is the first person to cross it and enter Paradise. The good believers cross it after that with a speed related to their good deeds. Some cross it in a glimpse, others like a shot arrow, others like a fast bird, others like a race-horse, others running, others walking, and the last people to cross it do so crawling.

Those who are destined to go to Hell are snatched down into it by hooks on the *sirat*. Believers who do not associate others with Allah but who have done evil deeds in their lifetime may also go to Hell, but are later forgiven and transferred to Heaven. Everyone in Heaven is given light in accordance with his good deeds.

We here believe the best approximation in terms of a translation of this Ayah is: *"Guide us to the Straight Path"*.

Chapter 10

صِرَاطَ ٱلَّذِينَ أَنْعَمْتَ عَلَيْهِمْ غَيْرِ ٱلْمَغْضُوبِ عَلَيْهِم وَلَا ٱلضَّآلِّينَ

Sirat Al-Latheen Anamta Alaihem Ghairi Al-Maghdhobi Alaihem wa la Adh-Dhaleen

The last aya in Al-Fatihah starts with the word *sirat*, i.e. way, road or path which we have already discussed in the previous aya. This aya explains further what is *as-sirat al-mustaqeem*. The first part of the aya says it is صراط الذين أنعمت عليهم *sirat al-latheen anamta alaihem*, i.e. it is the way or path of those whom You have favoured (or bestowed Your Grace upon).

There is an aya in the Quran which says:

وَمَن يُطِعِ ٱللَّهَ وَٱلرَّسُولَ فَأُوْلَٰٓئِكَ مَعَ ٱلَّذِينَ أَنْعَمَ ٱللَّهُ عَلَيْهِم مِّنَ ٱلنَّبِيِّـۧنَ وَٱلصِّدِّيقِينَ وَٱلشُّهَدَآءِ وَٱلصَّٰلِحِينَ وَحَسُنَ أُوْلَٰٓئِكَ رَفِيقًا ٦٩

(النساء/69)

"And whoever obeys Allah and the Messenger - those will be with the ones upon whom Allah has bestowed favor of the prophets,

126

the steadfast affirmers of truth, the martyrs and the righteous. And
excellent are those as companions"

Surat Al Nisa (Women), Ayah 69 [162]

The aya mentions four categories of favoured people in descending
order of closeness to the favours of Allah. So the person reciting the
last aya of Al-Fatihah is asking Allah to guide him on the path followed
by persons belonging to these four categories. Some interpreters say
that those favoured are such as the followers of Moses, before the
blessings of Allah deserted them. According to Ibn Abbas as related
by Ibn Juraij they are the *Mu'minoon* i.e. the believers, and according
to Wakee' they are the Muslims.

The next part of the aya says غير المغضوب عليهم *ghairi al-maghdhobi*
alaihem (pronounced ghairi-l-maghdhobi alaihem) i.e. not those who
incurred the wrath of Allah. Thus the persons favoured by Allah have
combined two favours: the favour of إيمان *iman* or faith, and the favour
of being safe from the anger of Allah. On the other hand a person who
incurs the wrath of Allah is one who is disobedient and who has been
deprived of the help of Allah.

Allah's anger with a person leads to Allah's wish to punish him. There
is a hadith which mentions the wrath of Allah and how alms-giving
extinguishes it:

إن الصدقة لتطفئ غضب الرب وتدفع ميتة السوء (رواه الترمذي)

i.e Indeed charity extinguishes the Lord's anger and it protects against
the evil death." (Narated by At-Tirmidhi). [163]

The wrath of Allah is mentioned in several ayas such as the following
two ayas:

إِنَّ ٱلَّذِينَ ٱتَّخَذُوا۟ ٱلْعِجْلَ سَيَنَالُهُمْ غَضَبٌ مِّن رَّبِّهِمْ وَذِلَّةٌ فِى ٱلْحَيَوٰةِ ٱلدُّنْيَا وَكَذَٰلِكَ نَجْزِى ٱلْمُفْتَرِينَ ﴿١٥٢﴾

النساء/69

"Indeed, those who took the calf (for worship) will obtain anger from their Lord and humiliation in the life of this world, and thus do We recompense the inventors (of falsehood)."

Surat Al-Ar'af, Ayah 152 [164]

And:

فَرَجَعَ مُوسَىٰ إِلَىٰ قَوْمِهِۦ غَضْبَٰنَ أَسِفًا قَالَ يَٰقَوْمِ أَلَمْ يَعِدْكُمْ رَبُّكُمْ وَعْدًا حَسَنًا أَفَطَالَ عَلَيْكُمُ ٱلْعَهْدُ أَمْ أَرَدتُّمْ أَن يَحِلَّ عَلَيْكُمْ غَضَبٌ مِّن رَّبِّكُمْ فَأَخْلَفْتُم مَّوْعِدِى ﴿٨٦﴾

(طه/86)

"So Moses returned to his people, angry and grieved. He said, "O my people, did your Lord not make you a good promise? Then, was the time (of its fulfillment) too long for you, or did you wish that wrath from your Lord descend upon you, so you broke your promise (of obedience) to me?"

Surat Taha, Ayah 86. [165]

Both these ayas are about Bani Israil, i.e. the Israilites or the Jews in the days of Moses who worshipped the calf and incurred the wrath of Allah. There is a long hadith related originally to Uday bin Hatem, part of which says:

128

Chapter 10: Sirat Al-Latheen Anamta Alaihem Ghairi Al-Maghdhobi Alaihem wa la Adh-Dhaleen

" الْيَهُودُ مَغْضُوبٌ عَلَيْهِمْ وَالنَّصَارَى ضُلَّالٌ " (رواه الترمذي)

"The Jews are those who Allah is wrath with, and the Christians have strayed." (Narated by At-Timidhi). [166]

Abdul Basit who is a present-day scholar says: "Even accepting the authenticity of this *hadith*, it only means that the Prophet mentioned these groups as examplesand did not in any way mean to exclude other groups" [167]

The last part of the aya is ولا الضالين *wa la adh-dhaleen* i.e. and neither those who are astray.

Aya 77 of Surat Al-Ma'idah is said by interpreters to refer to Christians. It says:

قُلْ يَا أَهْلَ الْكِتَبِ لَا تَغْلُوا فِى دِينِكُمْ غَيْرَ الْحَقِّ وَلَا تَتَّبِعُوا أَهْوَاءَ قَوْمٍ قَدْ ضَلُّوا مِن قَبْلُ وَأَضَلُّوا كَثِيرًا وَضَلُّوا عَن سَوَاءِ السَّبِيلِ ﴿٧٧﴾

(المائدة/77)

"Say, "O People of the Scripture do not exceed limits in your religion beyond the truth and do not follow the inclinations of a people who had gone astray before and misled many and have strayed from the soundness of the way.""

Surat Al-Ma'idah, Ayah 77. [168]

Thus those who incur the wrath of Allah are the disobedient and those who go astray are those who are ignorant about Allah. The person favoured by Allah combines the knowledge of the truth for its own

129

sake, and goodness for the purpose of doing it, and actually behaving according to it.

With this, this chapter concludes Al-Fatihah and therefore the last verse may be translated approximately as: *"The path of those whom You have bestowed upon Your blessings, not those who have earned Your Wrath, nor those who have gone astray (from the straight path)."*

Chapter 11

آمین

AMEEN

It is recommended for a person reciting Al-Fatihah to say آمین Ameen i.e. Amen. It is said that Ameen means: "Let it be so", and it is also said that it means: "O our Lord! Do with us as we have requested You" There is a *hadith* that says:

إذا قال الإمام "غير المغضوب عليهم ولا الضالين " فقولوا آمين فإنه من وافق قوله

قول الملائكة غفر له ما تقدم من ذنبه " (رواه النسائي وآخرون)

The Messenger of Allah (ﷺ) said: "When the Imam says: Not (the way) of those who earned Your anger, nor of those who went astray, say: 'Amin,' for if a person's Amin coincides with the Amin of the angels, his previous sins will be forgiven." [169]

There are differences of opinion between jurists regarding whether to say "Ameen" audibly or in your heart. Some (e.g. Abu Hanifa) say that if the imam says it audibly the congregation of persons praying should say it only in their hearts. But others (like Ahmed bin Hanbel, and Malek in one narrative related to him) say that the congregation should say it audibly, until the mosque vibrates (with the sound).

The Prophet ((ﷺ)) said:

" ما حسدتكم اليهود على شيء ما حسدتكم على السلام والتأمين" (رواه ابن ماجة)

i.e. "The Jews have envied you nothing as much as your saying *salam* and *ameen*" (related by Ibn Maja) [170]

According to some of the four Sunni Imams of Fiqh, saying ameen after the *imam* of the prayers when he completes reciting Al-Fatihah in the audible *rakaas* exempts a person praying after that *imam* from saying Al-Fatihah in his heart for that *rakaa*. In the Quran there is an aya in which Moses (PBUH) prayed to Allah, and in the following aya Allah answered that prayer to both Moses and his brother Harun (Aron) (PBUH), apparently because Harun was saying amen after Moses. The ayas say:

وَقَالَ مُوسَىٰ رَبَّنَآ إِنَّكَ ءَاتَيْتَ فِرْعَوْنَ وَمَلَأَهُۥ زِينَةً وَأَمْوَٰلًا فِى ٱلْحَيَوٰةِ ٱلدُّنْيَا رَبَّنَا لِيُضِلُّوا۟ عَن سَبِيلِكَ رَبَّنَا ٱطْمِسْ عَلَىٰٓ أَمْوَٰلِهِمْ وَٱشْدُدْ عَلَىٰ قُلُوبِهِمْ فَلَا يُؤْمِنُوا۟ حَتَّىٰ يَرَوُا۟ ٱلْعَذَابَ ٱلْأَلِيمَ ﴿٨٨﴾

"And Moses said, "Our Lord, indeed You have given Pharaoh and his establishment splendor and wealth in the worldly life, our Lord, that they may lead (men) astray from Your way. Our Lord, obliterate their wealth and harden their hearts so that they will not believe until they see the painful punishment."

قَالَ قَدْ أُجِيبَت دَّعْوَتُكُمَا فَٱسْتَقِيمَا وَلَا تَتَّبِعَآنِّ سَبِيلَ ٱلَّذِينَ لَا يَعْلَمُونَ ﴿٨٩﴾

Chapter 11: AMEEN

"(Allah) said, "Your supplication has been answered." So remain on a right course and follow not the way of those who do not know."

Surat Yunus, Ayat 88-89. [171]

So saying Ameen exempted Harun (Aron) from repeating the prayer of Moses (Peace of Allah be upon them both), as it was equivalent to saying it.

Conclusion

This book provides a relatively elaborate yet concise explanation of Al-Fatihah starting with a brief chapter about the Holy Quran, and from there takes the reader through the whole Al-Fatihah covering Al-Istiadah right through to the end with Ameen. No Muslim would ever claim that he could fully comprehend and fathom the depth of the meanings in Al-Fatihah and in the whole of the Quran. After all as the Almighty says:

هُوَ ٱلَّذِىٓ أَنزَلَ عَلَيْكَ ٱلْكِتَـٰبَ مِنْهُ ءَايَـٰتٌ مُّحْكَمَـٰتٌ هُنَّ أُمُّ ٱلْكِتَـٰبِ وَأُخَرُ مُتَشَـٰبِهَـٰتٌ ۖ فَأَمَّا ٱلَّذِينَ فِى قُلُوبِهِمْ زَيْغٌ فَيَتَّبِعُونَ مَا تَشَـٰبَهَ مِنْهُ ٱبْتِغَآءَ ٱلْفِتْنَةِ وَٱبْتِغَآءَ تَأْوِيلِهِ ۗ وَمَا يَعْلَمُ تَأْوِيلَهُۥٓ إِلَّا ٱللَّهُ ۗ وَٱلرَّٰسِخُونَ فِى ٱلْعِلْمِ يَقُولُونَ ءَامَنَّا بِهِۦ كُلٌّ مِّنْ عِندِ رَبِّنَا ۗ وَمَا يَذَّكَّرُ إِلَّآ أُوْلُواْ ٱلْأَلْبَـٰبِ ٧

آل عمران/7

"It is He who has sent down to you, [O Muhammad], the Book; in it are verses [that are] precise - they are the foundation of the Book - and others unspecific. As for those in whose hearts is deviation [from truth], they will follow that of it which is unspecific, seeking discord and seeking an interpretation [suitable to them]. And no one knows its [true] interpretation except Allah. But those firm in

knowledge say, "We believe in it. All [of it] is from our Lord." And no one will be reminded except those of understanding."
Surat Aal-Imran, Ayah 7 [172]

As such we can only explain what has been made accessible to us and and what we have been able to comprehend. It is only our faith which leads us to that belief which is required, regardless of how firmly grounded we are in our knowledge.

Al-Fatihah is the opening of the Quran and as explained in the earlier chapters, it has many names that reflect its order, content, functionality and value within the Holy Quran.

In as much as we very much hoped to highlight the most significant aspects of the sura, we also wanted to highlight the very significance of some of the key concepts of Islam, the Holy Quran and Al-Fatihah. We also hope that the book has been able to provide its reader with an insightful understanding of the core concepts of the Islamic creed presented so eloquently and concisely by the Almighty in Al-Fatihah.

As a conclusion to this book we offer here under our best approximation of the meanings of Al-Fatihah in English:

After *"I seek refuge in Thy Lord in the accursed Satan"*

أعوذ بالله من الشيطان الرجيم

(1) **In the Name of Allah, the Rahman (the source of endless and absolute Mercy), the Most Merciful;**

بِسْمِ اللَّهِ الرَّحْمَٰنِ الرَّحِيمِ ۜ ١

(2) **All absolute and perfect praise is only ultimately and truly attributed to Allah, the Master and Sustainer of all absolute existence (everything other than Allah);**

الْحَمْدُ لِلَّهِ رَبِّ الْعَالَمِينَ ٢

(3) *The Rahman, the Most Merciful;*

الرَّحْمَنِ الرَّحِيمِ ﴿٢﴾

(4) *Sovereign Master of the Day of Recompense;*

مَلِكِ يَوْمِ الدِّينِ ﴿٣﴾

(5) *It is You (and You) alone we worship and You (and You) alone that we ask for help;*

إِيَّاكَ نَعْبُدُ وَإِيَّاكَ نَسْتَعِينُ ﴿٥﴾

(6) *Guide us to the Straight Path,*

اهْدِنَا الصِّرَاطَ الْمُسْتَقِيمَ ﴿٦﴾

(7) *The path of those whom You have bestowed upon Your blessings, not those who have earned Your Wrath, nor those who have gone astray (from the straight path).*

صِرَاطَ الَّذِينَ أَنْعَمْتَ عَلَيْهِمْ غَيْرِ الْمَغْضُوبِ عَلَيْهِمْ وَلَا الضَّالِّينَ ﴿٧﴾

Ameen

آمين

When one reads many of the various translation, but more so when one reads the original verses in Arabic, one starts to realize the simplicity and depth of Al-Fatihah. This is an oft-repeated dialogue, a supplication and a prayer – and one where the central theme is pure tawheed (monotheism).

Al-Fatihah as one can see from the verses is Praise; calling upon the Lord in His grandest of attributes; accepting the fact that there shall be judgement by the Sovereign Master of the Universe, and as a consequence of that most just of judgements, the most accurate of dispensation of justice and absolute recompense. Then comes the very central theme: Al-Fatihah voids absolutely all types of intermediation between the servant and Master; between the supplicant and the Lord; between the worshiper and the Worshiped in *"It is You (and You) alone we worship and You (and You) alone that we ask for help"*.

The Quranic chapter ends with the ultimate request, the ultimate purpose of sincere prayer and the appeal from the created to the Creator and

Absolute Sovereign Master to lead them to the straight path, the path of the righteous who have been blessed and led to that path, not those who have rejected that righteous call and thus rejected salvation nor those who perhaps seek deliverance yet seek it whilst associating with Allah other deities/intermediaries or otherwise straying from the straight path by taking other paths not prescribed nor endorsed by the Almighty.

The Quran is a very momentous and rich book. Allah (SWT) says to the Prophet (ﷺ) in Surat Al-Muzzammil:

$$\text{إِنَّا سَنُلْقِى عَلَيْكَ قَوْلًا ثَقِيلًا ۝}$$

المزمل /5

"For we shall charge thee with a word of weight."
Surat Aal-Muzzammil, Ayah 5 [173]

We can sense this fact in a three verse sura like Al-Asr which says:

$$\text{وَٱلْعَصْرِ ۝}$$

$$\text{إِنَّ ٱلْإِنسَـٰنَ لَفِى خُسْرٍ ۝}$$

$$\text{إِلَّا ٱلَّذِينَ ءَامَنُوا۟ وَعَمِلُوا۟ ٱلصَّـٰلِحَـٰتِ وَتَوَاصَوْا۟ بِٱلْحَقِّ وَتَوَاصَوْا۟ بِٱلصَّبْرِ ۝}$$

العصر /1-3

(1) *"By Time"*
(2) *"Indeed, mankind is in loss"*
(3) *"Except for those who have believed and done righteous deeds and advised each other to truth and advised each other to patience"*.
Surat Al-Asr, Ayat 1-3 [174]

Conclusion

The first of the three ayas says: *"By Time"*. Some interpreters say that Allah is swearing by the afternoon, and some say He is swearing by the Asr prayer (i.e. afternoon prayer). But the interpreters generally favour the interpretation that Allah (SWT) is swearing by Time. The second aya says *"Indeed, mankind is in loss"*. This is because the life of a human being diminishes day after day between birth and death while he spends this life in persuit of worldly affairs and eventually it comes to an end. He would be a loser if after death he ends up in Hellfire.

The third aya says "Except for those who have believed and done righteous deeds and advised each other to truth and advised each other to patience." These four requirements together are necessary for a person to avoid being a loser and will enable him to gain a place in paradise. The first requirement is to believe that there is one and only one God, Allah, who is the Creater of everything and who has no partners whatsoever. But this is not enough, for even Iblis the Devil believed in Allah, the one and only God. This is clearly seen in the Quran itself; when Iblis was asked why he did not prostrate to the Lord's creation (Adam) he replied to Allah:

$$\text{قَالَ أَنَا۠ خَيْرٌ مِّنْهُ خَلَقْتَنِى مِن نَّارٍ وَخَلَقْتَهُۥ مِن طِينٍ ﴿٧٦﴾}$$

(ص/76)

"He said, "I am better than him. You created me from fire and created him from clay."

Surat Sad, Ayah 76 [175]

Thus a person has to fulfill the other conditions to deserve paradise. The second requirement is to live righteously including performing the *i'badat such as* Prayers, Fasting, Zakat, Haj, helping others etc. and abstaining from what Allah has forbidden such as drinking intoxicants and committing adultery and other major sins.

139

The third requirement is to advise each other to the truth and righteous deeds and avoiding wrong doings. The Quran states in Surat Al-Imran aya 110:

كُنتُمْ خَيْرَ أُمَّةٍ أُخْرِجَتْ لِلنَّاسِ تَأْمُرُونَ بِالْمَعْرُوفِ وَتَنْهَوْنَ عَنِ الْمُنكَرِ وَتُؤْمِنُونَ بِاللَّهِ وَلَوْ ءَامَنَ أَهْلُ الْكِتَبِ لَكَانَ خَيْرًا لَّهُم مِّنْهُمُ الْمُؤْمِنُونَ وَأَكْثَرُهُمُ الْفَسِقُونَ ۩

آل عمران/110

"You are the best nation produced [as an example] for mankind. You enjoin what is right and forbid what is wrong and believe in Allah. If only the People of the Scripture had believed, it would have been better for them. Among them are believers, but most of them are defiantly disobedient". Surat Aal-Imran, Ayah 110 [176]

Islam requires every Muslim to practice *da'wa* i.e. to deliver the message of Islam to others in the best way he could, through preacing in a wise way by words or by being a good example of a Muslim. We mentioned earlier in this book that the Prophet (ﷺ) said:

"بَلِّغُوا عَنِّي وَلَوْ آيَةً" (رواه البخاري وآخرون)

i.e. *"Convey from me even a (single) aya."* (Narrated by Al-Bukhari and others) [177]

The fourth and last condition to avoid being one of the losers and to deserve paradise is to practice patience and advise each other to practice it. This patience includes patience to perform what is right and avoid doing what is wrong. It is not enough to be good yourself but also necessary to encourage others to be righteous.

The Quran states:

وَمَاكَانَ رَبُّكَ لِيُهْلِكَ ٱلْقُرَىٰ بِظُلْمٍ وَأَهْلُهَا مُصْلِحُونَ ﴿١١٧﴾

هود/117

"And your Lord would not have destroyed the cities unjustly while their people were reformers". Surat Hud, Ayah 117 [178]

Thus in this short sura of 3 verses only we have guidance of how a person should live not to to gain the wrath of Allah and thus become a loser, but to gain the satisfaction and pleasure of Allah and be rewarded with paradise.

In Al-Kashaf, the classical interpretation of the Quran by Az-Zamakhshari there is a hadith in the interpretation of Surat Al-Asr attributed to the Prophet (ﷺ) that says:

" من قرأ سورة والعصر غفر الله له وكان ممن تواصى بالحق وتواصى بالصبر "

i.e. *He who reads Surat Al-Asr is forgiven by Allah and was one of those who advise each other to truth and advise each other to patience.* [179]

سورة العصر هي التي قال فيها الإمام الشافعي -رحمه الله-: "لو ما أنزل الله على خلقه حجة إلا هذه السورة لكفتهم" وقد شرح ابن القيم -رحمه الله- كلام الإمام الشافعي في كتابه مفتاح السعادة وذكره ابن القيم في التبيان ص53 وفي مفتاح دار السعادة 1 / 56

Surat Al-Asr is the one about which Imam Ash-Shafii, may Allah rest his soul, said: *"If Allah had not sent down to his creation except this sura then it would have sufficed"*. This saying by Imam Ash-Shafii was explained by Ibn Al-Qayyim, may Allah rest his soul, and was mentioned in his book At-Tibyan page 53 and in Miftah Dar As-Saada 1/56.

In concluding, we invite all those who have read this book to read the whole Quran, be they Muslims or Non-Muslims.

We pray to Allah to accept our modest effort and forgive any shortcomings in it, and bestow upon us His endless Mercy.

THE END

List of References and Author's Notes

Preamble

[1] Al Sahih International version as published on http://quran.com/. Surat Al-Baqarah (the Cow) – Ayah 143. *Note:* This original translation was used as the basis and some slight changes/additions were undertaken to enhance and improve the meaning by the authors. Here middle-nation was added with a just community placed in brackets; we replaced the people with mankind and the word Qiblah was capitalized.

[2] Al Sahih International version as published on http://quran.com/. Surat Al-Qasas, Ayah 4.

[3] Al Sahih International version as published on http://quran.com/. Surat Al-Duha, Ayah 77: Note: This original translation was used as the basis and some slight changes/additions were undertaken to enhance and improve the meaning by the authors. Here home was replaced with abode and desire was replaced with seek.

Introduction

[4] http://quran.al-islam.com/Loader.aspx?pageid=738&BookID=15&page=1 Surat Al Tawbah, Ayah 32.

[5] http://quran.al-islam.com/Loader.aspx?pageid=738&BookID=15&page=1 Surat Al Furqan, Ayah 32: Note: This original translation was used as the basis and some slight changes/additions were undertaken to enhance and improve the meaning by the authors: the word recited was added and placing rehearsed in brackets.

[6] Al Sahih International version as published on http://quran.com/. Surat Al-Alaq, Ayah 1-5.

[7] Hadith Related by Al-Bukhari, Sahih Al Bukhari. Reference: Sahih al-Bukhari 3; In-book reference: Book 1, Hadith 3; USC-MSA web (English) reference: Vol. 1, Book 1, Hadith 3 see: http://sunnah.com/bukhari/1/3.

Al-Fatihah

[8] Al Sahih International version as published on http://quran.com/. Surat Saba, Ayah 28: Note: This original translation was used as the basis and some slight changes/additions were undertaken to enhance and improve the meaning by the authors. Here universal messenger was added; glad was added and forewarner was added as opposed to warner.

[9] Al Sahih International version as published on http://quran.com/. Surat Al-Anbiya (The Prophets), Ayah 107.

[10] Al Sahih International version as published on http://quran.com/. Surat Al-Qalam (The Pen), Ayah 4.

[11] Al Sahih International version as published on http://quran.com/. Surat Al-Ma'eda, Ayah 67.

[12] Al Sahih International version as published on http://quran.com/. Surat Ash-Shu'ara', Ayah 214.

[13] Al Sahih International version as published on http://quran.com/. Surat Al-Ma'eda, Ayah 3. Note this is only part of the Ayah (Verse) being quoted.

[14] Al Sahih International version as published on http://quran.com/. Surat Al Saf, Ayah 9 & Al-Tawbah, Ayah 33. Note the word dieties was added after the word "others" and before the words "with Allah" to reflect closer meaning approximation.

[15] Hadith Related by Al-Bukhari, Sahih Al Bukhari. Reference: Sahih al-Bukhari 6943; In-book reference Book 89, Hadith 4, USC-MSA web (English) reference: Vol. 9, Book 85, Hadith 76. See http://sunnah.com/bukhari/89/4.

[16] Hadith no. (16998) 103/4 narrated by Ahmad bin Hanbal in his Musnad. See http://www.ahlalhdeeth.com/vb/showthread.php?t=157975

[17] Al Sahih International version as published on http://quran.com/. Surat Al Nahal (The Bee), Ayah58-59.

[18] http://hadith.al-islam.com/

[19] Al Sahih International version as published on http://quran.com/. Surat Al-Hijir, Ayah 9. Note the words "We will be its guardian" have been replaced with We will assuredly guard it (from corruption)" to reflect closer meaning approximation.

[20] The QURAN, (Full Quran Translation Text) Ali Unal; New Jersey, 2006. Surat Al Isra, Ayah 88. Note the word "though" has been replaced with "even if" to reflect closer and more accurate meaning approximation.

References and Author's Notes

[21] The Koran Interpreted. Translated with an introduction by Arthur J Arberry, Oxford University Press, World's Classic paperback, 1988, page 212

[22] The Koran Interpreted, Translated with an introduction by Arthur J Arberry, Oxford University Press, World's Classic paperback, 1988, page 201

[23] Al Sahih International version as published on http://quran.com/. Surat Al-Baqarah (The Cow) Ayah 79.

[24] Muhammad Rateb An-Nabulsi in his Arabic book "Wamadhat in Al-Islam, 4th section, paragraph (2-4): Khutbat Hijjat Al-Wada' (i.e. The Sermon of the Farewell Haj (of the Prophet PBUH)). See http://www.nabulsi.com/blue/ar/art.php?art=9503

[25] Al Sahih International version as published on http://quran.com/. Surat Al-Hujurat, Ayah 13.

[26] Al Sahih International version as published on http://quran.com/. Surat Fusilat, Ayah 53.

[27] Al Sahih International version as published on http://quran.com/. Surat Ibrahim, Ayah 4.

[28] Al Sahih International version as published on http://quran.com/. Surat Aal-Imran, Ayah 64: "Say: "O People of the Scripture, come to a word that is equitable between us and you - that we will not worship except Allah and not associate anything with Him and not take one another as lords instead of Allah". But if they turn away, then say, "Bear witness that we are Muslims [submitting to Him].".". Note: This original translation was used as the basis and some slight changes/additions were undertaken to enhance and improve the meaning by the authors to improve on the accuracy of the approximation.

[29] Al Sahih International version as published on http://quran.com/. Surat Yusuf (Joseph), Ayah 2.

[30] Al Sahih International version as published on http://quran.com/. Surat Fussilat, Ayah 44. Note the original translation is "And if We had made it a non-Arabic Qur'an, they would have said, "Why are its verses not explained in detail [in our language]? Is it a foreign [recitation] and an Arab [messenger]?" Say, "It is, for those who believe a guidance and cure." And those who do not believe - in their ears is deafness, and it is upon them blindness. Those are being called from a distant place." Additions were made to reflect closer meaning approximation.

Chapter 1: Legitimacy of the Translation of the Holy Quran

[31] Al Sahih International version as published on http://quran.com/. Surat Al-Isra, Ayah 29.

[32] The QURAN, (Full Quran Translation Text) Ali Unal; New Jersey, 2006;.. Surat Al Isra, Ayah 88.

[33] Al Sahih International version as published on http://quran.com/. Surat Al-Ahzaab (The Confederates) Ayah 39. Note the the authors replaced "Allah as Accountant" to "Allah to hold all to account". This slight change/addition was undertaken to enhance and improve the meaning by the authors to improve on the accuracy of the approximation.

[34] Al Sahih International version as published on http://quran.com/. Surat Al Nahal (The Bee), Ayah 125. Note the authors replaced "instruction" with "guidance (preaching). This slight change/addition was undertaken to enhance and improve the meaning by the authors to improve on the accuracy of the approximation.

[35] Hadith Narrated by Al-Bukhari, Sahih Al Bukhari.: Book 13, Hadith 5; Arabic/English book reference: Book 13, Hadith 1380. See: http://sunnah.com/riyadussaliheen/13/5

[36] Al Sahih International version as published on http://quran.com/. Surat Al-Zukhruf, Ayah 3.

[37] Al Sahih International version as published on http://quran.com/. Surat Yusuf (Joseph), Ayah 2.

[38] Al Sahih International version as published on http://quran.com/. Surat Al-Zumar, Ayah 28. Note that the word "crookedness" was added to improve the meaning and the accuracy of the approximation.

[39] Al Sahih International version as published on http://quran.com/. Surat Fusilat, Ayah 3. Note that the word "comprehend" was added to replace "know" to improve the meaning and the accuracy of the approximation.

[40] Al Sahih International version as published on http://quran.com/. Surat Al-Ra'd Ayah 37.

[41] The Holy Quran text, translation & commentary by Abdullah Yousuf Ali, published by Kamil Muslim Trust, first edition 1934; Surat Al Shu'ara, Ayah 195.

References and Author's Notes

Chapter 2: The Importance of Al-Fatihah

[42] Al Sahih International version as published on http://quran.com/. Surat Al-Hijr, Ayah 87.

[43] See Pages 59-60, Hadith No. 8: "Forty Hadith Qudsi" Selected and Translated by Ezzeddin Ibrahim & Denys Johnson-Davis, First published in 1976, and the edition published by the Islamic Texts Society 1997.

[44] Tafseer Al Quran Al 'Adheem (or Azheem), Dar Al Fikir Publishers and Distributors Al-Imam Abu Al Fida Al Hafid Ibn Katheer Al Dimashki.

[45] Sunan Ad-Darimi, Hadith Number 3236: See https://www.islamware. com/app/

[46] Tafseer Al-Fatihah Al Kabeer, Al Bahar Al Madeed, Part One, Authored by Imam Ahmed Bin Ajeebah (Arabic text), edited by Bassam Muhammad Barood, published by Al-Mujamma' Ath-Thaqafi, Abu Dhabi.

[47] See page 169, (The Prophetic Medicine), Ibn Al-Qayyim Al Jawjiyyah, rendered into English by S.Y. Abou Azar, Dar El Fiker, 1994.

[48] See page 8, (Tafseer Sura Al-Fatihah), Dr. Mohammed Ali Al Hasan, Al Risalah Foundation, Dar Al Basheer (Arabic text).

[49] See page 8, (Tafseer Sura Al-Fatihah), Dr. Mohammed Ali Al Hasan, Al Risalah Foundation, Dar Al Basheer (Arabic text).

[50] See page 7, (The Opening Chapter of the Qur'an) (Surah Al-Fatihah), Mawlana Abul Kalam Azad, edited and rendered into English by Dr. Sayed Abdul Latif, Islamic Book Trust Kuala Lumpur, (ibt books), 2001.

[51] See page 5 (The Essence of the Qur'an: Surah al-Fatihah), Abdul Basit, ABC International Group, Inc., KAZI Publications, 1997.

Chapter 3: Al-Istiadah or Seeking Refuge

[52] Al Sahih International version as published on http://quran.com/. Surat Al-Nahl, Ayah 98. Note that the word "read" was added to replace "recite" and the word "one" was added after the word "expelled" to improve the meaning and the accuracy of the approximation.

[53] Al Sahih International version as published on http://quran.com/. Surat Al-Kahf (The Cave), Ayah 50. Note that the word "(mention)" was removed to improve the meaning and the accuracy of the approximation.

[54] Al Sahih International version as published on http://quran.com/. Surat Sad, Ayah 76. Note that the word "Iblis" was added to improve the meaning and the accuracy of the approximation.

[55] Sunan Ibn Majah, The book of the Sunnah; English reference: Vol. 1, Book 1, Hadith 59; Arabic reference: Book 1, Hadith 62. See http://sunnah.com/urn/1250590.

[56] Muhammad Rateb An-Nabulsi: An-Nabulsi Encyclopedia of Islamic Uloom, lesson 126-127. See http://nabulsi.com/blue/ar/artp.php?art=3313

[57] Al Sahih International version as published on http://quran.com/. Surat Al-Baqarah (The Cow), Ayah 35-39. Note that the word "(dwellers)" and "(Hell)" were added in the 39th verse to improve the meaning and the accuracy of the approximation.

[58] Al Sahih International version as published on http://quran.com/. Surat Al-A'araf, Ayah 14-17. Note that the "allowed me to go astray" and "(to lure them from it)" were added in the 16th verse to improve the meaning and the accuracy of the approximation.

[59] Al Sahih International version as published on http://quran.com/. Surat Al-A'araf, Ayah 27.

Chapter 4: Al-Basmalah

[60] Islam website – managed by the Ministry of Islamic Affairs & Guidance, KSA. Surat An-Naml, (The Ants) Ayah 30. See:http://quran.alislam.com/Loader.aspx?pageid=738&BookID=15&page=1.

[61] Fiqh As-Sunnah by As-Sayyid Sabeq, Dar Al-Kitab Al-Arabi, Beirut, Lebanon.

[62] Bidayat Al-Mujtahed wa Nihayat Al-Muqtased by Ibn Rushd Al-Qurtubi, Dar Al-Kutub Al-Ilmiyah, Beirut, Lebanon, 10th edition, 1988.

[63] Al Sahih International version as published on http://quran.com/. Surat Fusilat, Ayah 53.

[64] Sahih al-Bukhari 6410, In-book reference: Book 80, Hadith 105, Sunnah.com

[65] Al Sahih International version as published on http://quran.com/. Surat Al Isra (The Assensation), Ayah 110. Note that the word "Ar-Rahman" was added and replaced "Most Merciful" to improve the meaning and the accuracy of the approximation.

[66] Al Sahih International version as published on http://quran.com/. Surat Al Furqan (The Criterian), Ayah 60. Note that the word "Ar-Rahman" was added and replaced "Most Merciful" (in two locations) to improve the meaning and the accuracy of the approximation.

[67] Al Sahih International version as published on http://quran.com/. Surat Al Furqan (The Criterian), Ayah 63. Note that the word "Ar-Rahman" was added and replaced "Most Merciful" (in two locations) to improve the meaning and the accuracy of the approximation.

[68] Ahmed bin Hanbal (died 241 H): Musnad Ahmed: Musnad the Ten Promised Paradise, Hadith number 1662, see http://hadith.al-islam.com.

[69] Al Sahih International version as published on http://quran.com/. Surat Al-Ahzab (The Confederates), Ayah 43.

[70] Al Sahih International version as published on http://quran.com/. Surat Al-Alaq, Ayah 1.

Chapter 5 - Al-Hamdalah

[71] The QURAN, (Full Quran Translation Text) Ali Unal; New Jersey, 2006;.

[72] Tafseer Al-Fatihah Al Kabeer, Al Bahar Al Madeed, Part One, Authored by Imam Ahmed bin Ajeebah, reviewed and edited by Bassam Muhammad Barood, published by Al-Mujamma' Ath-Thaqafi, Abu Dhabi, 1999 (Arabic text)

[73] See http://www.nobelprize.org/nobel_prizes/literature/laureates/1950/russell-lecture.htm

[74] Al Sahih International version as published on http://quran.com/. Surat Al-Dhariyat, Ayah 56.

[75] Al Sahih International version as published on http://quran.com/. Surat Saba, Ayah 1.

[76] Islam website – managed by the Ministry of Islamic Affairs & Guidance. Surat-Al-Fatihah, Ayah 1. See http://quran.al-islam.com/Loader.aspx?pageid=738&BookID=15&page=1

[77] Al Sahih International version as published on http://quran.com/. Surat Al An'am, Ayah 1. Note that the word "Yet" was added and replaced "Then" to improve the meaning and the accuracy of the approximation.

[78] Al Sahih International version as published on http://quran.com/ Surat Al Kahf (The Cave), Ayah 1. Note that the word "crookedness" was added to improve the meaning and the accuracy of the approximation.

[79] Al Sahih International version as published on http://quran.com/. Surat Saba, Ayah 1.

[80] Al Sahih International version as published on http://quran.com/. Surat Fatir, Ayah 1.

[81] Sayyid Abul A'la Mawdudi, Four Key Concepts of the Qur'an, The Islamic Foundation, Great Britain, 2006.

[82] Al Sahih International version as published on http://quran.com/. Surat Quyraish, Ayah 3-4.

[83] Al Sahih International version as published on http://quran.com/. Surat Al Shu'ara, Ayah 23-28.

Chapter 6 - Ar-Rahman Ar-Raheem

[84] Ibn Jareer At-Tabari (died 310 H): The Commentary on the Qur'an - Jami Al-Bayan fi Ta'wil al-Qur'an or Tafsir al-Tabari) (Arabic text)

[85] Al Sahih International version as published on http://quran.com/. Surat Al Kahf (The Cave), Ayah 1-2. Note that the word "crookedness" was added (in the first verse) to improve the meaning and the accuracy of the approximation.

[86] Al Sahih International version as published on http://quran.com/. Surat Al Baqarah (The Cow), Ayah 163. Note that the word "Rahman" was added to improve the meaning and the accuracy of the approximation.

[87] Al Sahih International version as published on http://quran.com/. Surat Al Naml (The Ants), Ayah 30. Note that the word "Rahman" was added to improve the meaning and the accuracy of the approximation.

[88] Al Sahih International version as published on http://quran.com/. Surat Fusilat, Ayah 2. Note that the word "Rahman" was added to improve the meaning and the accuracy of the approximation.

[89] Al Sahih International version as published on http://quran.com/. Surat Al Hashr, Ayah 22. Note that the word "Rahman" was added to improve the meaning and the accuracy of the approximation.

[90] Al Sahih International version as published on http://quran.com/. Surat Al-Isra (The Assensation) Ayah 110. Note that the word "Rahman (The Entirely Merciful)" was added to improve the meaning and the accuracy of the approximation.

[91] Sunan At-Tirmidhi, Hadith No. 3507.

[92] See Fatwa on-line: http://www.awqaf.gov.ae/Fatwa.aspx?SectionID=9&Ref ID=32869.

Chapter 7 - Maliki Yawm Ad-Deen

[93] Ahmed bin Hanbal (died 241): Musnad Ahmed bin Hanbal, hadith no. 180

[94] Al Sahih International version as published on http://quran.com/. Surat Aal-Imran Ayah 26. Note that the words "You have full power over everything" replaced "You are over all things competent" to improve the meaning and the accuracy of the approximation.

[95] Al Sahih International version as published on http://quran.com/. Surat Al Nas, Ayah 2.

[96] Al Imam Mohammed Bin Ali Bin Mohammed Al Shawkani (died in 1255 H) - Quran interpretation - Fatih Al Qadeer – Al Jamme bayn Fannai Ar-Riwayah wa A-Dirayah min Elm Al Tafseer, Dar Zamzam (Publisher) – Al Riyadh – KSA; 1255 Hijri; (Arabic text)

[97] Al Ghazali – The ninety-Nine Beautiful Names of God (Al-Maqsad Al-Asna fi Sharh Asma Allah Al-Husna) Translated with Notes by David B. Burnell and Nazih Daher (first published in 1992 by the Islamic Texts Society), ISBN-0946621-31-4.

[98] Ibn Jareer At-Tabari (died 310 H): The Commentary on the Qur'an - Jami Al-Bayan fi Ta'wil al-Qur'an or Tafsir al-Tabari) (in Arabic)

[99] Abu Abdullah Muhammad bin Ahmed Al-Ansari Al Qurtubi (died 671 H): "Al-Jam' li Ahkam Al-Quran wa Al-Mubayyen li ma Tadhamman min As-Sunnah wa Ahkam Al-Furqan" a classical tafsir of the Quran (Arabic text)

[100] Sheikh Muhammad Abduh (1849-1905), Tafsser Al Quran Al Hakeem – AKA "Tafseer Al Manar" (Arabic Text) – Vol 1; Al Imam Sheikh Muhammed Abduh – Written by Sayed Muhammad Rashid Rida (Founder of Al Manar); Dar Al Maarifah for Printing and Distribution – Lebanon;

Al-Fatihah

[101] Al Sahih International version as published on http://quran.com/. Surat Al Haj, Ayah 47.

[102] Al Sahih International version as published on http://quran.com/. Surat Al Sajdah, Ayah 5.

[103] Al Sahih International version as published on http://quran.com/. Surat Al Maarij, Ayah 4. Note that the word "measure" replaced "extent" to improve the meaning and the accuracy of the approximation.

[104] The QURAN, (Full Quran Translation Text) Ali Unal; New Jersey, 2006;. See page 697.

[105] The QURAN, (Full Quran Translation Text) Ali Unal; New Jersey, 2006;. See page 854.

[106] Al Sahih International version as published on http://quran.com/. Surat Al-Isra (The Assensation) Ayah 19.

[107] Al Sahih International version as published on http://quran.com/. Surat Aal-Imran Ayah 114.

[108] Mawlana Adul Kalam Azad: The Opening Chapter of the Quran (Sura Al-Fatihah); Rendered into English by Dr. Syed Abdul Latif; Islamic Book Trust-KL (IBT); 2001/1962.

[109] Al Sahih International version as published on http://quran.com/. Surat Al-Jathiyah, Ayah 21-22.

[110] Sheikh Muhammad Abduh (1849-1905): Tafsser Al Quran Al Hakeem – AKA "Tafseer Al Manar" (Arabic Text) – Vol 1; Al Imam Sheikh Mohammed Abdoh – Written by Sayed Muhammad Rashid Rida (Founder of Al Manar); Dar Al Maarifah for Printing and Distribution – Lebanon;

[111] Al Sahih International version as published on http://quran.com/. Surat Al-Infitar, Ayah 9.

[112] THE GLORIOUS QURAN (Full Quran Translation Text); Text Translation and Commentary, Abdul Majid Daryabadi; The Islamic Foundation, 2003/1424 Hijri. Surat Al Zalzalah, Ayat 8-9.

[113] Sheikh Muhammad Abduh (1849-1905), Tafsser Al Quran Al Hakeem – AKA "Tafseer Al Manar" (Arabic Text) – Vol 1; Al Imam Sheikh Muhammad Abduh – Written by Sayed Muhammad Rashid Rida (Founder of Al Manar); Dar Al Maarifah for Printing and Distribution – Lebanon;

References and Author's Notes

[114] Al Sahih International version as published on http://quran.com/. Surat Az-Zalzalah, 8-9

[115] Al Sahih International version as published on http://quran.com/. Surat Fusilat, 46.

[116] Fourty Hadith Qudsi; Selected and Translated by Ezzeddin Ibrahim and Denys Johnson-Davis, The Islamic Texts Society, 1997.

[117] Al Sahih International version as published on http://quran.com/. Surat Al Baqarah (The Cow), Ayah 286.

[118] "Maalem At-Tanzeel" (or Tafsir Al Baghawi); Abu Muhammad al-Husain ibn Masood al-Baghawi, (born 433 H or 436 H – died 516 H/1122 AD). 4th edition, 1997, published by Dar Taiba tor Publication and Distribution, Riyadh, Saudi Arabia.

[119] Al Sahih International version as published on http://quran.com/. Surat Az-Zukruf, Ayah 87.

[120] Duroos Min Al Quaran (Arabic Text); Al Imam Al Sheikh Muhammed Adbuh (1849 -1905/1266-1323 H); Dar Ihya Al Uloom, Beirut, Leboanon 2nd Edition 1981 (1401 H).

[121] Al Sahih International version as published on http://quran.com/. Surat Al-Hijr, Ayah 49-50.

[122] Sahih al-Bukhari 6463, In-book reference: Book 81, Hadith 52, USC-MSA web (English) reference: Vol. 8, Book 76, Hadith 470. See http://sunnah.com/bukhari/81/52.

[123] The Holy Quran – Translations of Selected Verses; Martin Lings (Abu Bakar Suraj-ul Deen); The Royal Aal Al-Bayt Institute for Islamic Thought & The Islamic Texts Society; 2007.

Chapter 8 – Iyaka Na'budu wa Iyaka Nasta'een

[124] The QURAN, (Full Quran Translation Text) Ali Unal; New Jersey, 2006

[125] Taqi Addin Ahmed bin Taymiyyah (born 661 H) "Minhaj (i.e. The Clear Way of) the Prophet's Sunna in refuting the arguments of the Shiites and Qadaris"

[126] The Tafsir of the Quran by Sheikh Muhammad Mutwali Ash-Sharawi. (in Arabic).

Al-Fatihah

[127] Islam website – managed by the Ministry of Islamic Affairs & Guidance (Saudi Arabia), Surat Al-Furqan, Ayah 63-65. See http://quran.al-islam.com/Loader.aspx?pageid=738&BookID=15&page=1

[128] Al Sahih International version as published on http://quran.com/. Surat Al Baqarah (The Cow), Ayah 186. Note that the word "[O Muhammad]" has been removed to attain the accuracy of the approximation.

[129] Al Sahih International version as published on http://quran.com/. Surat Az-Zukhruf, Ayah 68.

[130] Al Sahih International version as published on http://quran.com/. Surat Sa'ad, Ayah 82-83.

[131] Al Sahih International version as published on http://quran.com/. Surat Az-Zumar, Ayah 53.

[132] Al Sahih International version as published on http://quran.com/. Surat Al-FurqanA(The Criterion) Ayah 17.

[133] Al Sahih International version as published on http://quran.com/. Surat Al- Anfal, Ayah51 & Surat Aal-Imran, Ayah 182.

[134] Al Sahih International version as published on http://quran.com/. Surat Al- Dharriyat, Ayah 56.

[135] Islam website – managed by the Ministry of Islamic Affairs & Guidance (Saudi Arabia). Surat Al Mu'minon, Ayah 115.

See http://quran.al-Islam.com/Loader.aspx?pageid=738&BookID=15&page=1.

[136] Al Sahih International version as published on http://quran.com/. Surat Hud, Ayah 61.

[137] Islam website – managed by the Ministry of Islamic Affairs & Guidance (Saudi Arabia). Surat Qaf, Ayah 16.

See http://quran.al-islam.com/Loader.aspx?pageid=738&BookID=15&page=1.

[138] Al Sahih International version as published on http://quran.com/. Surat Al-Iklas Ayah 1-4. Note that the word "begotten" was added to the 3rd verse to ensure better accuracy of the approximation.

[139] Al Sahih International version as published on http://quran.com/. Surat Al-Anbya, Ayah 22.

[140] Al Sahih International version as published on http://quran.com/. Surat Al-Baqarah (The Cow), Ayah 165.

[141] Al Sahih International version as published on http://quran.com/. Surat Al-Nisa (Women), Ayah 48.

[142] Al Sahih International version as published on http://quran.com/. Surat Al-Nisa (Women), Ayah 116.

[143] Al Sahih International version as published on http://quran.com/. Surat Al-Bayinah, Ayah 6.

[144] Al Sahih International version as published on http://quran.com/. Surat Aal-Imran, Ayah 31.

[145] Al Sahih International version as published on http://quran.com/. Surat Al-Tawbah, Ayah 24.

[146] Hadith narrated by Al-Bukhari - Arabic/English book reference: Book 1, Hadith 183. See http://sunnah.com/riyadussaliheen/1/183.

[147] Hadith narrated by Al-Bukhari - Arabic/English book reference: Book 13, Hadith 1380. See http://sunnah.com/riyadussaliheen/13/5.

[148] Al Sahih International version as published on http://quran.com/. Surat Aal-Imran, Ayah 104.

[149] Hadith – Narrated by Al Tirmidhi: An-Nawai's Forty Hadtth, Translated by Ezzedin Ibrahim and Denys Johnson-Davies, The Holy Koran Publishing House, Damascus, 1967 Arabic/English book, Hadith 19

Chapter 9 - Ihdina As-Sirat Al-Mustaqeem

[150] Al Sahih International version as published on http://quran.com/. Surat Al-Balad, Ayah 8-10.

[151] Al Sahih International version as published on http://quran.com/. Surat Al-Kahf (The Cave), Ayah 17.

[152] Al Sahih International version as published on http://quran.com/. Surat Al-A'araf Ayah 30.

[153] Al Sahih International version as published on http://quran.com/. Surat Al-Ankabut (The Spider), Ayah 69. Note that the word "(i.e. in Our cause)" has been added to attain the accuracy of the approximation.

Al-Fatihah

[154] Al Sahih International version as published on http://quran.com/. Surat Al-Qasas, Ayah 56.

[155] Al Sahih International version as published on http://quran.com/. Surat Ash-Shuraa, Ayah 52.

[156] Al Sahih International version as published on http://quran.com/. Surat Al-Mu'minun, Ayah 74.

[157] Hadith in Jami` at-Tirmidhi, Chapters on Parables. See http://www.sunnah.com

[158] Hadith - Sunan Abi Dawud 4719, In-book reference: Book 42, Hadith 124, English translation: Book 41, Hadith 4701. See http://sunnah.com/abudawud/42/124.

[159] Al Sahih International version as published on http://quran.com/. Surat Aal-Imran, Ayah 8.

[160] Hadith narrated by Bukhari & Muslim, Arabic/English book reference: Book 1, Hadith 588. See http://sunnah.com/riyadussaliheen/1/588.

[161] Hadith narrated by Muslim, Sahih Muslim 2822, In-book reference: Book 53, Hadith 1. See http://sunnah.com/muslim/53/1.

Chapter 10 - Sirat al-Latheen Anamt Alaihem; Ghairi Al-Maghdoob Alaihem Wala Ad-Daleen

[162] Al Sahih International version as published on http://quran.com/. Surat Al-Nisa (Women) Ayah 69.

[163] Hadith - Jami` At-Tirmidhi, Al-Jami As-Sahih, Hadith no. 664, (in Book 7, hadith 48). See http://sunnah.com/tirmidhi/7/48.

[164] Al Sahih International version as published on http://quran.com/. Surat Al-Ar'af, Ayah 152.

[165] Al Sahih International version as published on http://quran.com/. Surat Taha, Ayah 86.

[166] Hadith in Jami Al Tirmidhi - Arabic reference: Book 47, Hadith 3212 - English reference: Vol. 5, Book 44, Hadith 3954 as in http://sunnah.com/urn/739380.

[167] See page 71 (The Essence of the Qur'an: Surah al-Fatihah), Abdul Basit, ABC International Group, Inc., KAZI Publications, 1997.

[168] Al Sahih International version as published on http://quran.com/. Surat Al-Ma'idah, Ayah 77.

Chapter 11 - Ameen

[169] Hadith – from Sunan an-Nasa'i 929, In-book reference: Book 11, Hadith 54, English translation: Vol. 2, Book 11, Hadith 930. See http://sunnah.com/nasai/11/52.

[170] Hadith – from Sunnan Ibn Majah, English reference: Vol. 1, Book 5, Hadith 856, Arabic reference: Book 5, Hadith 905. See http://sunnah.com/urn/1309040.

[171] Al Sahih International version as published on http://quran.com/. Surat Yunus, Ayah 88-89.

Conclusion

[172] Al Sahih International version as published on http://quran.com/. Surat Aal-Imran, Ayah 7.

[173] Mohammed Mormaduke Pickthall, Holy Quran, English Translation, Madras House, London: Surat Al Muzzammil, Ayah 5.

[174] Al Sahih International version as published on http://quran.com/. Surat Al-Asr, Ayah 1-3.

[175] Al Sahih International version as published on http://quran.com/. Surat Sad Ayah 76.

[176] Al Sahih International version as published on http://quran.com/. Surat Aal-Imran, Ayah 110.

[177] Hadith Narrated by Al-Bukhari, Sahih Al Bukhari.: Book 13, Hadith 5; Arabic/English book reference: Book 13, Hadith 1380. See: http://sunnah.com/riyadussaliheen/13/5

[178] Al Sahih International version as published on http://quran.com/. Surat Hud, Aya 117.

[179] Al Kashshaf – 'An Haqeq Ghawamedh At-Tanzeel Wa Uyoon Al Aqaweel fi Wujood At-Taweel' – Vol. 1, by Al Imam Abu Al-Qaseem Jar-Allah Mahmood bin Omar Bin Muhammad Az-Zamakshari (468-538 H); published by Dar Al Kitaab Al-Arabi, Beirut, (Arabic Text).

END OF REFERENCES

Printed in the United States
By Bookmasters